Busy Brides

Bible

ning a fabulous wedding, without
e expensive cost of a wedding planner.

Angela A. Kear

Llumina Press

ISBN: 978-1-60594-431-9

Printed in the United States of America by Llumina Press

Library of Congress Control Number: 2010903032

Angela A. Kear Bio

Angela A. Kear is originally from Buffalo, New York. She currently lives in Columbia, South Carolina as a freelance writer. In 2002 she graduated magna cum laude from the State University of New York College at Buffalo with a Bachelor's of Science degree. She also works as a visual merchandiser for Lacoste/24-Seven in South Carolina.

Mrs. Kear has over ten years of event planning, marketing, sales, photography, and wedding experience, including planning her own fabulous wedding two years ago. She is a detail-oriented person with a passion for perfection. She has experienced every aspect of the wedding world from being a guest, bridesmaid, bride, photographer, venue site coordinator, and a wedding planner. She has done it all, loves it all, and has incorporated it all into her book, *The Busy Bride's Bible for planning a fabulous wedding, without the expensive cost of a wedding planner.*

Bible Contents

One

The Engagement

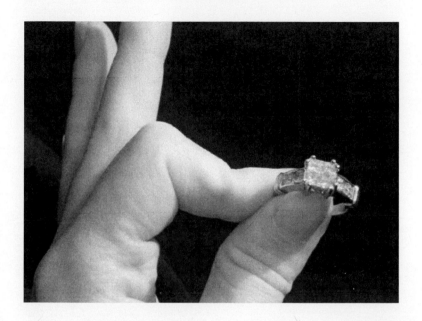

The engagement, or promise to marry, is the period between the day of the proposal and the day of the marriage. The Western engagement tradition is to place a ring on the woman's left-hand ring finger to symbolize an agreement for future marriage.

Busy Bride, now that you're engaged, your first step is to show off that fabulous ring. Wear it, and wear it proud. Some couples also choose to send out an engagement announcement to all their friends and family.

Your second step is to set up an appointment for your engagement photograph. The photograph will be added to your engagement announcement and sent to all your local newspapers.

Your third step is setting up the engagement party. Some couples send invitations for a more formal party, and some couples call by phone and invite their guests for a more casual party. A formal party might take place in a rented room of a restaurant; whereas a casual party might take place in someone's home or backyard. Either way, the bride's parents generally pay for the engagement party.

The engagement party is a great opportunity to get everyone together, especially if both sets of parents have not yet met each other. Remember, this is only the beginning of the wedding planning process, and the better everyone gets along the easier the process.

Don't rush the engagement period . . . relax. Most couples wait a year to a year and a half before they get married.

❖ Busy Bride ❖ Stop. Don't include your wedding gift registry in your engagement party invitation. If your engagement party guests choose to bring a gift that is completely their choice.

Two

Busy Bride's Ten Commandments

1. Start your wedding planning process by purchasing a three-ring binder and plastic sheets to create your wedding organizer. While planning your wedding, you need to remember to place everything wedding related in the binder. Dividers are helpful in keeping your wedding organizer in order.

2. Never leave an appointment with a vendor without getting what you want. Remember, it is your money and your wedding.

3. Always ask for everything to be put in writing when working with your vendors.

4. When you're feeling stressed out, you should review all the wedding planning items that you have completed. Reviewing all your wedding planning accomplishments will give you the strength and the perseverance to continue with your wedding plans. Also, periodic massages, facials, manicures, pedicures, and physical exercise will help relieve the stress in your mind, body, and soul.

5.   Organize, organize, organize . . . Being organized is a necessity when planning a fabulous wedding.

6.   Sometimes in life it's okay to be last minute, but when planning a wedding being last minute is not an option.

7.   Delegate, delegate, delegate . . . If you have 200 invitations to put together, or wedding programs that need to be folded, call someone to help. For example, some grandmothers love to feel helpful and needed. As a token of your gratitude for her help, you can mention a special thank you to her and her help in your rehearsal dinner or reception toast.

8.   Watch your wedding budget closely because a little over here and a little over there can be a large overage in the end.

9.   Get creative. Don't settle for an ordinary wedding. Make your wedding an extraordinary event that you, your family, and your friends will remember forever.

10.   No matter what goes wrong, be happy and enjoy your wedding day.

Three

Busy Bride's Dos And Don'ts

Dos:

❖ Do read the fine print on all your vendors' contracts before you sign any. Get educated about contract signing.

❖ Do keep in mind what a wedding really is. The main event is your ceremony, and your reception is the celebration party. Put extra thought into the readings, music, and vows for your ceremony because this will make your ceremony as memorable as possible.

❖ Do call all the guests who have not responded by RSVP. Call no later than two weeks before the wedding.

❖ Do put a family member or friend in charge of watching your gift table, especially if your wedding reception is outside.

Don'ts:

* Don't open your gifts at your reception.

* Don't decide not to send a wedding invitation to guests who have already received a save-the-date. If you mailed them a save-the-date, you must mail them a wedding invitation.

* Don't freeze-dry your bouquet or boutonnieres, let your photos and video show the beauty of your flowers. Don't spend the extra money for dead dried-up flowers, you can't reuse them.

* Don't expect a perfect wedding day, things will go wrong. Aim for perfection, but settle for memorable.

* Don't leave a wedding appointment without a receipt and a copy of any contract you signed. Anytime you spend your wedding money or sign your name, you should have a written document, or contract, to protect yourself from any future mistakes or misunderstandings.

* Don't give a photograph of you (Busy Bride) and your groom to your guests as your

wedding favor. This makes you and your groom look self-centered, conceited, and extremely full of yourselves. A guest favor is a gift to your guests for them to enjoy.

❖ Don't use your place cards as your wedding favor to your guests. Think about your guests, do you think they really want a mini frame or mini chair with their names in it or on it? This type of favor is useless to your guests.

❖ Don't get trashed the night before your wedding. Don't let your friends or your groom's friends plan the bachelorette or bachelor parties for the night before your wedding. The last thing you need, Busy Bride, is for you or your groom to wake up hung over on the biggest day of your lives— your wedding day.

Four

Wedding To-Do Timeline

Congratulations!
Busy Bride, you're engaged!

Make sure you do the following:

- ✓ Choose your engagement ring
- ✓ Take engagement portrait to give to the newspapers
- ✓ Organize your engagement party
- ✓ Send out your engagement party invitations
- ✓ Announce your engagement to the local newspapers in both yours and your fiancé's cities
- ✓ Enjoy your engagement party
- ✓ Send out thank-you cards to guests you received gifts from
- ✓ Start attending local bridal shows and expos

Twelve or more months before the wedding, you should begin making these preparations:

- ✓ Purchase a three-ring wedding binder and plastic sheets to create your wedding organizer
- ✓ Place everything wedding related in the binder
- ✓ Discuss how wedding expenses will be distributed among all paying parties
- ✓ Determine your wedding budget
- ✓ Decide on your wedding theme
- ✓ Determine your wedding formality
- ✓ Determine the type of wedding ceremony
- ✓ Determine a wedding ceremony location site
- ✓ Visit at least ten or more reception sites
- ✓ Determine the season and time of day you would like to hold your wedding
- ✓ Choose a reception site and reserve your wedding date and time
- ✓ Choose a wedding color palette
- ✓ Decide on the size of your wedding
- ✓ Draft initial guest list
- ✓ Finalize guest list
- ✓ Decide on a wedding officiant or clergyperson, then meet with your chosen officiant or clergyperson to schedule the wedding time and date, and to discuss ceremony details
- ✓ Sign up for premarital counseling
- ✓ Shop for, select, and order wedding rings

- ✓ *For a destination wedding only,* select and order wedding stationery (save-the-dates, invitations, RSVPs, thank-you cards, ceremony programs, etc.), then mail your save-the-date cards
- ✓ Determine desired honeymoon location
- ✓ Apply for passports (if needed for foreign travel)
- ✓ Start planning reception
- ✓ Shop for a photographer or videographer or both

Nine to twelve months before the wedding:

- ✓ Shop for and decide on a wedding dress, headpiece, shoes, then place your order
- ✓ Shop for, choose, and order maid or matron of honor's and bridesmaids' attire
- ✓ Choose a photographer or videographer or both, then reserve him, her, or them for your wedding time and date
- ✓ Choose a DJ or live entertainment or both, then reserve whomever you chose for your wedding time and date
- ✓ Shop for, choose, and reserve a catering company (if not provided by your reception site)
- ✓ Shop for, choose, and reserve a beverage service company (if not provided by your reception site or caterer)

- ✓ Determine the menu with the catering company
- ✓ Book honeymoon and pay first down payment (never pay in full too far in advance)
- ✓ Shop for a florist (remember to bring along photos of the ceremony and reception sites)
- ✓ Choose a florist and place initial order
- ✓ *For a local wedding,* now you can select and order wedding stationery (save-the-dates, invitations, RSVPs, thank-you cards, ceremony programs, etc.), then mail your save-the-date cards
- ✓ Choose and order ceremony accessories (unity candle, ring bearer's pillow, flower girl's basket, rose petals or rice, aisle runner, etc.)
- ✓ Choose and order reception accessories (personalized napkins, drink stirrers, cake boxes, cookie or candy bags, toasting glasses, wedding favors, cake server set, guest book or frame, cake topper, pen set, etc.)

Six months before the wedding:

- ✓ Shop for and choose a wedding cake designer; sign contract and place order
- ✓ Choose and hire wedding day transportation services
- ✓ Attend premarital counseling
- ✓ Help mother and future mother-in-law select wedding attire

- ✓ Receive bridal gown delivery
- ✓ Select and order groom's attire
- ✓ Select and order groomsmen's attire
- ✓ Get marriage license application information from the county clerk's office, a church, state authority, or other area-issuing agency in the location where you plan to marry
- ✓ Confirm date and time with ceremony site, reception site, caterer, florist, photographer, videographer, DJ or band, ceremony musicians, cake designer, and transportation services
- ✓ Set up bridal gift registries at two or more stores

Three months before the wedding:

- ✓ Begin bridal gown alterations
- ✓ Purchase bridal garter, under garments, jewelry, veil, gloves, purse, etc.
- ✓ Schedule and attend bridesmaids' dress and shoe fittings
- ✓ Research wedding hotel accommodations and directions for out-of-town guests
- ✓ Create a wedding direction card and a list of local hotel accommodations for out-of-town guests (these will be mailed to any out-of-town guests who RSVP that they are attending)

✓ Prepare all wedding invitations

✓ Hire calligrapher, if necessary, to address invitation envelopes

✓ Set appointment, if necessary, for submitting marriage license application (do this one month before wedding date)

✓ Order gifts for all attendants (bride's and groom's)

✓ Create a "must photograph" list for photographer

✓ Create a schedule for DJ or live band, include your "must play" list and what to announce when

✓ Meet a second time with wedding officiant and confirm all ceremony details

✓ Schedule bridal shower location, date, and time for about two months before the wedding date

✓ Prepare and mail all bridal shower invitations

✓ Schedule bridal portrait for two months before the wedding date

Two months before the wedding:

✓ Schedule and attend final fitting for bridal gown with shoes and all accessories

✓ Mail all wedding invitations

✓ Schedule ceremony rehearsal location, date, and time

✓ Schedule rehearsal dinner location, date, and time

✓ Pick up finished bridal gown
✓ Attend bridal portrait sitting
✓ Order address labels with your new name and address (for thank-you cards)
✓ Design your wedding ceremony program
✓ Purchase a special gift for your fiancé. This will be given to him before your ceremony on your wedding day
✓ Schedule a hair appointment for a wedding hair trial run at your hair salon
✓ Schedule wedding day hair appointments for you (bride), bridal attendants, mother of the bride, fiancé's mother, and anyone else who needs one
✓ Attend bridal shower
✓ Prepare and mail all bridal shower gift thank-you cards
✓ Make hotel reservations for your wedding night
✓ Meet with the photographer to review the wedding itinerary for your wedding day and your "must photograph" list. Give the photographer copies of both
✓ Meet with the DJ or live band to review the wedding itinerary for your wedding day, your "must play" list, and announcements

One month before the wedding:

- ✓ If you are providing your own bar, stock it by purchasing all the bar essentials listed under the wedding beverage section
- ✓ Assemble wedding favors
- ✓ Start making a log of all gifts received and from whom, send thank-you cards promptly after the gift is received
- ✓ Mail all rehearsal ceremony and dinner invitations
- ✓ Start logging all RSVPs for the wedding as they are received. Start a guest count
- ✓ Choose bridal portrait and have it framed for display on your wedding day
- ✓ Review wedding day itinerary and confirm all dates and times with ceremony site, reception site, clergyperson or wedding officiant, caterer, florist, photographer, videographer, DJ or live band, ceremony musicians, cake designer, transportation service, all attendants, and all other needed parties
- ✓ Print wedding ceremony programs
- ✓ Schedule and meet with your professional makeup artist, if you have one, for a wedding day trial run. Purchase all cosmetics needed for your wedding day
- ✓ Schedule appointment with your makeup artist for your wedding day. If you're

applying your own makeup, purchase all your wedding cosmetics and start wearing the makeup regularly so that you can get used to it and make adjustments before your wedding day

✓ Schedule your manicure and pedicure appointment for the day before your wedding or the day of the wedding rehearsal for you, your bridal party, your mother, your fiancé's mother, and anyone else who needs one

✓ Mail bridal portrait (5x7) and wedding announcement to all the local newspapers in both yours and your fiancé's cities. Make sure the newspapers know to print your announcement on the first Sunday after your wedding day, or you can wait until after the wedding and send a bride and groom portrait with your announcement to the newspapers

✓ Collect all information and documents required to apply for your marriage license. Don't forget to bring your fiancé

✓ Apply for your marriage license at the county clerk's office, a church, state authority, or other area-issuing agency in the location where you plan to be married

Two weeks before the wedding:

- ✓ Call all rehearsal ceremony and dinner invites and confirm attendance
- ✓ Call all guests who you have not received RSVPs from to confirm attendance at the wedding
- ✓ Create reception seating chart with a sketch
- ✓ Attend your bachelorette party, while your groom attends his bachelor party

One week before the wedding:

- ✓ Finalize guest count with reception site and caterer
- ✓ Finalize order with florist
- ✓ Call and confirm all hair, manicure and pedicure, and makeup appointments
- ✓ Drop off wedding gown at bridal shop for its final steaming
- ✓ Start packing for the honeymoon, especially if you're leaving directly after the wedding for it
- ✓ Pack wedding day attire

Two days before the wedding:

- ✓ Pick up your bridal gown from the bridal shop. Bring a king-size flat white sheet to

wrap the gown in. This will help keep it from wrinkling and protect it from getting dirty
- ✓ Pack what you will need for your wedding night
- ✓ Finish packing for your wedding day, wedding night, and honeymoon

One day before the wedding:

- ✓ Attend manicure and pedicure appointment
- ✓ Attend rehearsal ceremony and dinner
- ✓ Meet with ushers and review their roles in the ceremony
- ✓ Prep any last minute details or changes
- ✓ Relax and rest for the big day

The wedding day:

It's the day you have been dreaming of, your wedding day . . .

After the wedding:

- ✓ Prepare and mail all wedding gift thank-you cards

Enjoy your honeymoon!

Five

The Budget

oday's weddings cost a HUGE amount of money, anywhere from twenty thousand dollars to thirty thousand dollars on average. Every bride's first step in planning her fabulous wedding is to determine her total wedding budget, and who is paying for what. I recommend coming up with an estimate of how much money you will need for the wedding. Then meet with all the paying parties to see what each is able to contribute. Traditionally, the bride's parents were responsible for paying for the whole wedding. Times have changed and that isn't always the case now. Below is a recommended list of who generally pays for what at a wedding.

Bride:
- Groom's ring
- Her attendants' gifts

Groom:
- Bride's rings
- His attendants' gifts

Bride's family:
- ❖ Reception
- ❖ Stationery
- ❖ Flowers
- ❖ Bridal attire
- ❖ Photography
- ❖ Entertainment
- ❖ Transportation
- ❖ Some miscellaneous fees

Groom's family:
- ❖ Rehearsal dinner
- ❖ Wedding officiant's fees
- ❖ Groom's attire

Bride's attendants:
- ❖ Their own attire
- ❖ Bridal shower
- ❖ Bachelorette party

Groom's attendants:
- ❖ Their own attire
- ❖ Bachelor party

Keep in mind that this is just a suggested guideline, and it can be altered depending on each paying party's financial situation. Also, sometimes different cultures have different, or altered, customs for who pays for what. Just as long as someone pays, that's all that matters.

❖ **Busy Bride** ❖ stop. Look for money saving tips throughout this book that will help you to cut costs and save you from wedding inflicted bankruptcy.

❖ **Busy Bride** ❖ stop. Earn freebies by shopping for your wedding with a credit card that rewards you for using it. Some credit cards give you cash back like Discover Card, some give you free reward gifts like Bank of America, and some give you frequent flier miles like Capital One. So my advice is to search for the best deal for you and take full advantage of all the freebies.

Below is a sample outline to show you how to split up your total wedding budget into categories. It also shows what is in each category and the budgeted percentage for each. You may decide to spend less in one category and more in another, that's fine. The choice is yours.

Sample Total Wedding Budget with a budgeted percentage for each category:

Reception—50%
For reception site, rehearsal dinner, beverages, caterer, cake, rental items, etc.

Bride's and Groom's attire—10%

For bridal gown, veil, headpiece, hosiery, undergarments, shoes, accessories, jewelry, hair styling, makeup, groom's tuxedo or suit, shoes, tie, cuff links, studs, suspenders, etc.

Flowers—10%

For all flowers, wedding decorations, etc.

Photography—10%

For the photographer's or videographer's or both their fees, additional prints, albums, videos

Entertainment—7%

For ceremony and reception music, the DJ's or entertainment's (live band, comedian, jugglers, etc.) fees or both their fees

Transportation—3%

For wedding party transportation and guest transportation (if transporting guests)

Stationery—2%

For save-the-dates, wedding invitations, response cards, thank-you cards, stamps, guest book, etc.

Rings—3%

For wedding bands and engraving (if desired)

Miscellaneous Fees—5%

Wedding officiant's fees, attendants' gifts, wedding guest favors, cake serving set, candles, unforeseen costs, etc.

Busy Bride, if your total wedding budget is ten thousand dollars, then the reception, including the rehearsal dinner, should cost five thousand dollars or less. That's fifty percent of your total wedding budget. When choosing a total wedding budget always choose less than you can afford because ninety-nine percent of most brides go over their budget. For example, if you can afford a twelve thousand dollar total wedding budget, then start with ten thousand dollars and leave the two thousand dollars for upgrades, add-ons, fees, and miscellaneous wedding must haves.

Also, notice that the engagement ring and honeymoon are not included in the total wedding budget. These items are typically paid for by the groom, and they are not items that are directly part of the wedding day event.

After you have calculated the amounts for each category, you may want to revise the percentages according to your priorities. Once you have a set clear-cut wedding budget total and the exact amounts you can spend in each category, stick to it. If you go over in one category try to compensate for the overage by going under in another.

Ask for wedding deals and discounts. Let your vendors know you have a budget and see if they can provide a deal or discount. Most likely they will be able to work with you and your budget, if not, they're not worth your time or money.

❖ **Busy Bride** ❖ stop. Save money by getting together with friends and family to review your budget categories to see if anyone you know has any wedding related connections. These connections can save you a HUGE amount of money. For example, if a family member owns a flower shop, he or she may be able to service your wedding at half the cost.

Six

Wedding Themes

First, before you can begin buying or planning, you need to determine your fabulous theme and decide what time of year (season) you want to get married. For example, if you're interested in a beach themed wedding you need to plan it for the spring or summer, not the freezing winter months. Your wedding theme can incorporate your heritage, hobbies, religion, pets, culture, or any type of favorites in your life.

❖ **Busy Bride** ❖ stop. Your work is done. Below are some examples of wedding theme ideas:

- ❖ Fall or autumn theme (orange and natural décor)
- ❖ Fantasy or fairy tale theme
- ❖ Holiday theme (Valentine's Day, Saint Patrick's Day, Halloween, or your favorite holiday)
- ❖ Beach theme (tropical, seashells, nautical, luau, etc.)
- ❖ Animal theme (butterfly, fish, puppies, doves, dolphins, etc.)

- Cultural or ethnic theme (Italian, Irish, Asian, Jewish, Hispanic, etc.)
- Las Vegas or casino theme
- Country or wild west theme
- Sports fan theme
- Hollywood glamour theme
- Celebrity replica theme (your favorite actor, entertainer, athlete, etc.)
- Celebrity impersonator theme (Elvis, Marilyn Monroe, Dolly Parton, Cher, etc.)
- Organic or go green theme
- Winter wonderland theme
- Destination theme
- Mardi Gras theme
- Masquerade ball theme
- Garden theme
- College or fraternity or sorority theme
- Lake theme
- Boat theme
- Nightclub theme
- Movie theater theme
- Carnival theme
- Religious theme
- Disney theme
- Favorite movie or TV show theme
- Zoo or safari theme
- Location inspired theme (Italy, Australia, Paris, England, etc.)
- Circus theme

- Pirate theme
- Gothic theme
- Patriotic theme
- Military theme
- Victorian theme
- Redneck theme
- Any other creative theme that you consider *fabulous . . .*

Keep in mind, your wedding theme should customize your wedding day. The theme should give character and creativity to your day.

Seven

Wedding Formality Guide

Now that you have determined your wedding budget and theme, the next step is to determine your wedding formality. The number of guests you're going to invite, the time and location of the ceremony and reception, and the bride's and groom's attire all play a role in determining your wedding formality. Below are the four main degrees of wedding formality. Once you have decided on your wedding formality degree, this will then help you decide other essential elements of your wedding, such as your bridal gown style.

Ultra Formal

Number of guests invited—300 or more

Time of day—evening (5 PM or later)

Locations:

Ceremony—a religious indoor ceremony at a house of worship

Reception—at a mansion, hotel ballroom, country club, resort, etc.

Bride's attire:

Bridal gown—a floor length gown with very elaborate peal beading, crystals, or embroidery. Example styles are ball gown and A-line/princess

Train—cathedral length train

Headpiece—very elaborate tiara or crown

Veil—cathedral length veil

Gown fabric—silk, satin, fine lace, tulle, or chiffon

Groom's attire:

Black tailcoat tuxedo, matching trousers, white wing-collared shirt, patent leather shoes, studs, cufflinks, and gloves

---

Formal

Number of guests invited—100–300

Time of day—late afternoon (3–5 PM)

Locations:

Ceremony—a religious or civil indoor ceremony

Reception—at a rented banquet hall, historical building, art gallery, conference center, etc.

Bride's attire:

Bridal gown—a floor length gown with peal beading, crystals, or embroidery. Example styles are ball gown, A-line/princess, mermaid, and empire

Train—chapel or sweep length train

Headpiece—tiara or crown

Veil—chapel or fingertip length veil

Gown fabric—satin, organza, fine lace, or charmeuse

Groom's attire:

Black tuxedo, bow tie, vest or cummerbund, white tuxedo shirt, and cufflinks

---

Semi-Formal

Number of guests invited—100 or less

Time of day—early afternoon (12–3 PM)

Locations:

Ceremony—a religious or civil, indoor or outdoor ceremony

Reception—cruise ship, beach club, waterfront restaurant, rooftop, botanical gardens, etc.

Bride's attire:

> **Bridal gown**—a long or short length gown. Example styles are mermaid, column, and empire
>
> **Train**—chapel length train
>
> **Headpiece**—not always worn. Examples are simple comb, barrettes, or headband
>
> **Veil**—fingertip or elbow length veil
>
> **Gown fabric**—taffeta, lace, brocades, or shantung

Groom's attire:

> Formal suit, white dress shirt, cummerbund or vest, and tie

---

Informal

> **Number of guests invited**—50 or less
>
> **Time of day**—any daytime hour

Locations:

> **Ceremony**—a civil indoor or outdoor ceremony
>
> **Reception**—backyard, fire hall, private home, public park, lodge, etc.

Bride's attire:

Bridal gown—simple floor length, tea length, or shorter. Example styles are casual dress or knee length suit

Train—not usually worn

Headpiece—not always worn. Examples are wreath, flower circle, single flower behind the ear, or flower hair clip

Veil—not usually worn

Gown fabric—cotton or linen

Groom's attire:

Business suit, white dress shirt, and tie. Ultracasual groom's attire would be khakis and linen white shirt

---

❖ **Busy Bride** ❖ stop. Help your groom look his best. If your groom loves his beer and his belly shows it, help him hide the gut with a vest and not a cummerbund. Also, darker colors are more slimming, so stay away from bright colors or large patterns. Busy Bride, remember, the more gorgeous your groom looks, the more beautiful you look.

❖ **Busy Bride** ❖ keep in mind that the formality of the wedding should set the tone for the entire wedding event. So choose the degree of formality that best fits your wedding day vision and incorporate it throughout the wedding planning process.

Avoid mixing and matching degrees of formality; this will only confuse your guests. You want your guests to have a clear-cut idea of the degree of formality so they will know what they are expected to wear.

Eight

Local Bridal Shows And Expos

Bridal shows and expos are fabulous events for busy brides to attend and shop for local wedding resources. They're one-stop shopping events for busy brides in the wonderful world of wedding planning. Busy brides can meet, ask questions, and collect a great amount of information directly from wedding professionals. Bridal shows and expos generally showcase the latest wedding trends, from wedding dress styles to transportation options to signature drinks and dessert bars. These events are a fabulous way for busy brides to get ideas, information, prices, and education on the amount of services their local wedding professionals can provide.

Many exhibitors will provide demonstrations, samples, free drawings, special event rates, free promotional gifts, and much much more. The best part is, even if there is a small admission fee, the entire show and expo is full of wedding freebies. So take advantage of it. Not many things are free in the wedding world.

Start searching for local bridal shows and expos twelve to eighteen months before your wedding, or I recommend as soon as you become engaged. Your local newspapers and bridal wedding magazines are generally where these events are advertised. Another option is to search the Internet for local upcoming bridal shows and expos; you can almost always find something online. If your city is too small to host any type of bridal show or expo, you might need to search larger cities near you.

In addition to the exhibitors' booths, most bridal shows and expos have some type of music and wedding fashion show. The fashion show generally spotlights the latest in the wedding world. Don't forget to bring along your groom, mother, and as many bridesmaids you can gather. They also need to learn about the fashion forward wedding trends and how to take an active role in helping you, Busy Bride, plan the largest event of your life . . . your wedding.

Prepare to feel overloaded with wedding materials by the end of the event. Keep in mind that you have a year or more to plan your wedding, so you don't have to decide everything in a day. Take it one bridal step at a time. Don't stress, take as many information materials home as you possibly can from the event and review later. Keep the ones you want to call, and recycle the rest.

❖ Busy Bride ❖ stop. The number one rule when attending bridal shows and expos is this—never sign any type of contract on site. Exhibitors might try to tell you a special price is only good that day if you sign a contract at the event, but don't believe them. Most exhibitors will offer that same price in their place of business. Keep in mind that the best wedding professionals are not the ones generally hurting for business. It is the new, or just plain bad, wedding professionals. Either way, I recommend following my number one rule.

Attend as many bridal shows and expos as your schedule permits. Busy Bride, remember, the more educated you are about the wedding world, the smarter you will be when you spend your time and money planning your wedding.

For the next year or more, planning your wedding is going to take up a large amount of your time so make it enjoyable, from the bridal shows and expos to the dress fittings to the vendor appointments and much much more. Make every minute a memorable wedding planning memory.

Now enjoy as many bridal shows and expos as possible.

Nine

Ceremony Sites

The wedding ceremony is the most important part of the wedding day. During the ceremony the bride and groom exchange vows or profess their love for one another in front of all their family and friends.

The time of day that you hold this special event is one of the first things to consider when planning your wedding day. Most wedding ceremonies occur in the afternoon in order to have natural daylight for photographs and enough time for a cocktail hour, dinner, dancing, and celebration.

Determining your type of wedding ceremony is generally a simple choice if both you and your fiancé have similar religious backgrounds; however, if they are different, you will need to find a happy medium. The four most popular types of wedding ceremonies are religious, civil, military, and nontraditional.

The number one most common type of wedding ceremony is religious. When both bride and groom are the same religion, then this ceremony is an easy option. However, choices will need to be made if you and your fiancé are of different faiths and you both want a religious ceremony. Now, more and more faiths are working together and finding a happy medium with an inter-faith wedding ceremony. Some religions are even allowing couples to have both officiants marry them at the same time. Not all faiths are as accepting of other faiths as some are, so check with your officiant. Another choice is to have two wedding ceremonies, one representing each of your faiths. In some situations this is the best of both worlds.

A second type of wedding is a civil ceremony. Usually a civil wedding ceremony is performed by a judge, justice of the peace, marriage commissioner, or even a cruise ship captain. Most civil wedding ceremonies take place outside of the church. Civil wedding ceremonies can be just as classy, romantic, and elegant as a religious wedding ceremony. Some are large, some are small, some are inside, and some are outside, but every one of them is special in some way.

A third type of wedding is a military ceremony. One partner has to be in the military, or retired, in order to choose this option. You also have the option of utilizing a military chapel as your ceremony site. Generally, the military spouse-to-be will dress in his or her dress uniform.

The other officers present will also dress in uniform and create an arch of swords for the new couple to walk under after the ceremony. As the bride walks through, the last two officers with swords gently touch their swords to the bride's behind or block the couple and make them kiss.

A fourth type of wedding is a nontraditional ceremony. This wedding ceremony is similar to a civil wedding ceremony, but generally includes more religious aspects because either the bride or groom is a member of a nontraditional faith. This wedding ceremony is performed by a wedding officiant who recognizes that faith and includes many religious elements, allowing the couple to have the most power over the creation of their own wedding ceremony.

Once you and your fiancé have decided on the type of wedding ceremony, or ceremonies, you both want, the next step is to meet with your officiant. Discuss your location options, like do you have to get married in a church or can the ceremony be conducted on a beach, garden, or other location.

❖ ꝑusy ꝑride ❖ stop. Your work is done. Below is a list of wedding ceremony sites for you to consider using for your wedding:

- ❖ Church or house of worship
- ❖ Mountain top or cliff

- Ski slope
- Beach
- Yacht, cruise boat or speed boat
- Mansion
- Mall or department store
- Public park
- River or lake or waterfall
- Government building or historical monument
- Museum
- Apple or other orchard
- Garden
- Rooftop
- Private home or backyard
- Location where you first met
- College campus
- Sporting event
- Zoo
- Lodge
- Casino
- Las Vegas chapel
- Supermarket
- Airport or airplane or helicopter
- Roller rink or skate park
- Bowling alley
- Nightclub
- Movie theater
- Hot air balloon
- On jet skies
- On four-wheelers

- ❖ On horseback or at a horse ranch
- ❖ Farm
- ❖ Fast food restaurant
- ❖ Fair or festival
- ❖ Theme park or carnival ride
- ❖ Gas station

❖ Busy Bride ❖ stop. You need to consider any rules, regulations, permits, restrictions, parking rules, or other items that might need to be addressed once you have chosen a wedding ceremony site.

After you, the groom, and officiant have decided on a location, the next step is to start reviewing the ceremony details and plans. Busy Bride, keep in mind that the more extraordinary the wedding ceremony site, the more memorable the ceremony. So be creative.

Ten

Reception Sites

Location, location, location . . .

The reception site, or venue location, is one of the most important aspects of your wedding. Before you start scheduling appointments at different sites, take a moment to think about your wedding formality, theme, budget, number of invites, and your ideal vision for the site.

Once you and your groom have reviewed the elements above, then you can start making your appointments to visit all the possible reception sites. Treat each appointment as though you are interviewing the reception site to see if the location meets all your criteria. I recommend visiting at least ten or more venue sites before you make your final decision. Treat this process as though you are shopping for one of the most important purchases of your wedding . . . because it is.

❖ Busy Bride ❖ start looking as early as possible for your reception site. I recommend you start looking at least twelve months or more before the wedding. Reception sites book quickly, especially the fabulous ones. So as soon as you receive your engagement ring, start looking. As soon as you decide on a reception site, book it and avoid losing it.

Location, location, location . . . words real estate agents live by, but I also consider them wedding words of wisdom. Finding that one fabulous location for your reception is one of the most important aspects in creating a fabulous dream wedding. Don't settle for ordinary, because every bride deserves only the extraordinary on her wedding day.

Today there are endless reception site locations, so be creative and think outside the box. Below is a list of both traditional wedding reception sites and some unique ones that will "wow" your guests:

- At home or backyard
- Planetarium
- Art gallery or museum
- Sports stadium or roller rink or race track or bowling alley
- Auditorium or convention center or conference center
- College
- Banquet hall
- Cruise ship or boat or yacht
- Plantation
- Country club
- Beach or beach club
- Country inn or a bed and breakfast
- Loft
- Historical village or historical building
- Resort (on a mountain, near ocean, etc.)
- Rooftop garden, public or private garden, greenhouse, public park
- Winery
- Movie theater
- Zoo
- Farmhouse or barn or ranch
- Waterfront restaurant
- Casino
- Camp grounds or fair grounds

- ❖ Lighthouse
- ❖ Nightclub
- ❖ Mansion
- ❖ House of worship hall
- ❖ Hotel ballroom
- ❖ School gym
- ❖ Fire hall
- ❖ Apple or other fruit orchard
- ❖ Opera house
- ❖ Castle
- ❖ Amusement park

❖ **Busy Bride** ❖ keep in mind that the reception site is where all your guests will come together and celebrate your new beginning as a married couple. So it should be coordinated to match with the same formality and tone of your ceremony.

❖ **Busy Bride** ❖ also keep in mind that your reception budget is no more than fifty percent of your total wedding budget. The reception budget includes the site rental, food, beverages, cake, rental items, and any other expenses associated with the reception cost.

❖ **Busy Bride** ❖ stop. Your work is done, so read below. These are the questions you should ask when you're interviewing, or shopping, for a reception site:

1.   What is the reception site rental fee?
2.   What does the reception rental fee include?
3.   What dates and times are available?
4.   What is the maximum number of guests the site can accommodate for a seated reception?
5.   What is the maximum number of guests the site can accommodate for a cocktail reception?
6.   Does the reception site provide catering services or do you need to bring in your own caterer?
7.   If the reception site provides catering services, what is the price range for food?
8.   Can you taste test the food selection before you make your decision to sign a contract?
9.   What areas at the reception site are going to be available to your guests?
10. What is the amount of time the site will be available to you and your guests?
11. Does the site provide dinnerware, table, linens, or chairs?
12. Is there room for a dance floor? If so, where?
13. What will be the ratio of servers to guests?

14. Does the site have a liquor license? If yes, ask to see a copy of the license. If not, do you have to obtain a one-day special license?

15. Does the site have liability insurance? If yes, ask to see a copy.

16. If the reception site provides beverage services, what types of bar packages does the site provide?

17. Do you supply the liquor or does the site? Who furnishes the bartenders?

18. Ask if your wedding will be the only wedding for the day or will there be others.

19. Ask to see the health department permit, recent inspection and score, and insurance certificates. Make sure they are current.

20. How many bathrooms are on site for your guests? (Check all the bathrooms out. A good rule of thumb is at least two bathrooms per 100 guests.)

21. Ask if the site has an in-house or on-site cake designer?

22. If you bring a cake from an outside vendor, does the site charge a cake cutting fee?

23. Does the site charge a fee for parking or valet service?

24. Ask if there is a ceremony area on site. If yes, then ask what the fee is for using it.

25. Does the site have a changing room for the bridal party?

26. Are there guest accommodations nearby?
27. Does the site have a coatroom, or can one be set up?
28. What is the deposit amount, and when is the remainder due?
29. Does the site have any noise restrictions?
30. Does the site allow musical entertainment on site, such as a DJ or band?
31. What are the decoration guidelines?
32. Does the site have a list of recommended vendors who they typically work with?
33. If it is an outdoor site, what alternative plans does the reception site have in case of bad weather?
34. What is the typical table reception layout?
35. How many people can each table seat?
36. Is there a room set aside for taking photographs?
37. How many wedding ceremonies and receptions does the site host per year?
38. Is the bridal suite available on site? If yes, is it free for the bride and groom?
39. In the event of a natural disaster, will the reception site reschedule the event for free or is there a charge? If so, what is the charge?
40. What are the site's payment, cancellation, and refund policies?

Finding your dream reception site is a lot like finding your dream home. In both cases, when you see it, you will know it's right. Follow your instincts and be confident in your decision, but don't forget to ask the questions I've provided.

Once the reception site has been evaluated, has passed all your interview questions, and you feel confident that this site is the one, the last question you need to ask is to review the reception site's contract.

❖ *Busy Bride* ❖ stop. Wait to sign the contract. Take it home and read it over first. Make sure it contains the essential elements below:

1. Wedding date, start, and end times
2. Your names (Busy Bride and Groom), venue site name, and manager's name
3. Reception areas being rented at the site (main ballroom, garden area, outside courtyard, etc.)
4. Total cost with line-by-line items and the number of guests included
5. Deposit amount
6. Items (tables, linens, chairs, etc.) provided by the site
7. List of rental items (vases, candles, etc.) and prices
8. A payment worksheet
9. Cancellation and refund policy

10. Proof of site liability insurance and liquor license if providing liquor
11. Any site usage restrictions (music, alcohol, noise issues, etc.)
12. Any additional terms you have orally agreed upon. Always get oral promises in writing, don't rely on just a handshake

Now that you have everything in writing, you and your groom can sign and date the contract along with the reception site manager, and pay the deposit. Make sure you receive a copy of the entire contract with yours, your groom's, and the reception site manager's signatures. This contract now represents your guarantee of services and fees between you and your reception site. I think of it as your written protection against any surprises.

Once you have finished with the contract, I recommend taking out your camera and shooting away. Photograph everything from the entrance, signs, restrooms, parking lot, reception room, and art on the walls. Shoot in front of the site and anywhere else you can think of. You will need these photographs later for when you make your final decisions on the wedding formality, theme, color palette, flowers, seating chart, and more.

Make your wedding an event to be remembered. Don't think ordinary, think extraordinary. Busy Bride, your wedding reception is the first major event hosted by you and your new husband, so make it memorable by personalizing it with your own fabulous style as a couple. Create memories that will last a lifetime, for you and your guests.

Eleven

The Wedding Date

When choosing the date of your wedding, keep in mind your wedding theme, color palette, flowers, ceremony site, and reception site. All are important factors in creating your dream wedding. Some couples choose a special date, such as the day they met or maybe a holiday they both enjoy. I recommend staying away from the big holidays like Christmas, Thanksgiving, and Easter. These holidays are too busy to give your wedding the proper attention it deserves.

❖ **Busy Bride** ❖ stop. You can save money by choosing a date during the off-peak wedding season. The peak wedding season lasts from June until September. About forty-five percent of each year's weddings are during these months. I recommend the month of May, because you can utilize the wonderful spring flowers and colors, and still stick to your budget.

Think about your family and attendants and check with their schedules. Make sure you don't choose a date that conflicts with anyone's schedules, unless it's a family member you really don't want at your wedding! You can tell that family member it was the only day available at the ceremony or reception site.

Once you have a date in mind, check with your ceremony and reception sites to make sure they are both available on your chosen date. Don't choose a date or time of year that is a busy time at work for you or your groom. For example, if you're an accountant, choosing a date during tax season is out of the question, unless you plan to quit your job prior to the wedding. I don't recommend doing that.

Should you choose Friday or Saturday? That depends on your situation. A Friday wedding is generally cheaper, but your guests may not be able to get away from work to attend on time, or at all. A Saturday wedding is generally more expensive, but your guests won't have to rush from work. Each situation is different, so make the decision that best suits your needs.

Don't debate too long on the date. Choose a date, book it with your vendors, and start creating your save-the-dates.

Twelve

Wedding Color Palette

After you have chosen the location, date, and theme of your wedding, visualize the ceremony and reception sites with and without decorations. Next, rule out what colors will clash with the current location colors. For example, if the site has dark colored walls or carpet than pastels or cool colors will not work. If you forget what colors are at the ceremony and reception sites, then make an extra appointment to take some photos of the areas. Use these photos with paint sample chips from your local hardware store to help determine your fabulous wedding color palette. Keep in mind that a wedding color palette generally has three colors: one dominant color, one subordinate color, and one accent color. Cut the paint sample chips into small squares and sort them into three-color palette combinations. Once you have chosen a color palette combination, glue all three paint chip squares on a piece of cardboard. You can then take the three paint chip color combination, which is now your wedding color palette, to all your wedding appointments. This will help coordinate the exact same color palette throughout the wedding.

When incorporating your color palette, remember the essential items your guests will notice first, such as the invitations, attire, flowers, cake, favors, and table linens. These are all very visible elements at the wedding, so use your chosen wedding color palette when adding color to any of these highly visible wedding elements.

❖ Busy Bride ❖ stop. Don't overdo it with color. Sometimes less is better, and too much is tacky. Below are examples of some of my favorite wedding color palettes.

Dominant	+	Subordinate	+	Accent Colors
Red	+	gold	+	white
Red	+	gold	+	cream
Red	+	silver	+	white
Red	+	silver	+	cream
Burgundy	+	gold	+	white
Pink	+	sliver	+	white
Pink	+	gold	+	cream
Pink	+	brown	+	cream
Fuchsia	+	black	+	white
Fuchsia	+	lime	+	white
Violet	+	lilac	+	white
Violet	+	lilac	+	lime
Jade	+	pink	+	butter
Deep blue	+	yellow	+	white
Deep blue	+	lilac	+	white
Tiffany blue	+	black	+	white
Aqua	+	gold	+	white
Aqua	+	brown	+	white

❖ **Busy Bride** ❖ stop. Another option is to determine your wedding color palette by season. Choose one or two colors from the season and use black, white, cream, gold, or silver as your subordinate or accent colors. Below is an example list of wedding colors organized by seasons:

- **Summer** (hot and cool colors)—hot pink, fuchsia, lavender, mango orange, lime, turquoise
- **Spring** (bright bold colors)—red, yellow, green, blue, chocolate browns
- **Fall** (fall or autumn colors)—dark red, mustard yellow, pumpkin orange, deep green, camel, beige, taupe, rust, brown, gold
- **Winter** (coral colors)—pink, blue, silver, winter white, black

Don't forget to choose a wedding color palette at least twelve months or more before the wedding. Stay on track by following the wedding to-do timeline; this will ensure a fabulous wedding that is well planned and organized.

Use your wedding colors as another chance to express yourselves as a couple. Make sure you choose a wedding color palette that fits your personalities. Don't be afraid to be bright and bold with your color choices. Keep in mind that the more one-of-a-kind your wedding, the more meaningful and memorable.

Thirteen

Guest List

Never start orally inviting people until you have them on a written guest list. Think about what you and your groom's wedding vision includes. Does it include a huge guest list or a smaller more intimate guest list? Then divide the guest list total by one-third for the bride's parents to invite, one-third for the groom's parents to invite, and one-third for the bride and groom to invite. This way both sets of parents can create their lists, and you and your groom can create your list together. Gather all three lists and do the numbers. Keep in mind that thirty to forty percent of the guests invited will generally decline.

Have all three parties then create a second list of potential guests who did not make their first list, but could be invited if there is enough room. Utilize that second list of guests to fill those empty spots as they become available. I recommend starting your guest lists as early as possible, at least twelve months before the wedding.

❖ Busy Bride ❖ stop. You can utilize your guest lists even after your wedding is over. The proper etiquette is to send a holiday card for the first Christmas or Hanukkah or holiday after your wedding to each family on your guest list. To create an extra fabulous card, add a holiday photo of you and your husband, so your guests can see how well you're doing as a couple.

Below are some guest list "don'ts" to live by when planning your wedding guest list:

1. Don't invite any friends you haven't seen in the last three years. Family is the one exception to this rule.

2. Don't invite ex-wives, ex-husbands, ex-boyfriends, ex-girlfriends, ex-baby daddies, or ex-baby mommas unless you and your groom are both comfortable with the guest.

3. Don't invite acquaintances.

4. Don't invite guests without sending them an invitation. It's just wrong.

5. Don't photocopy the invitation. If you run out, order more invitations, or don't invite any additional guests.

Utilize the guest list template below to organize your guest list and keep track of what has been completed.

Guest List Template

Name:_____

Address:_____

City:_____State:_____Zip:_____

Home phone:_____

Cell phone:_____

E-mail:_____

- ❖ Invitation mailed_____
- ❖ RSVP received_____
- ❖ Number of guests confirmed attending_____
- ❖ Gift received_____
- ❖ Thank-you card mailed_____

❖ **Busy Bride** ❖ stop. Be prepared. Always purchase twenty percent more invitations than you actually need to mail. This will compensate for any invitation clerical errors when writing names and addresses, and it will also allow for some extra invites, maybe from that second guest list.

Planning ahead makes life less painful and stressful in the end.

Fourteen

Save-The-Dates

S ave-the-dates are announcements you send to your guests as a preliminary invitation to your wedding. Your save-the-dates should coordinate with your wedding theme, color palette, and other wedding stationery pieces. Today, there are many types of save-the-dates:

- ❖ Standard cards
- ❖ Postcards
- ❖ Magnets
- ❖ Chocolate bars
- ❖ Snow globes (winter wonderland theme)
- ❖ Messages in a bottle (beach or destination theme)
- ❖ New Year's noisemakers
- ❖ Mardi Gras beads (Mardi Gras theme)
- ❖ Leis (tropical theme)
- ❖ Flip-flops (beach theme)
- ❖ Bottles of green beer (Saint Patrick's Day theme)
- ❖ Playing cards (Las Vegas or casino theme)
- ❖ Masquerade masks (masquerade ball theme)
- ❖ Heart-shaped cookies (Valentine's Day theme)
- ❖ Calligraphed or inscribed pumpkins (autumn or Halloween theme)

- ❖ Beer koozies (college theme)
- ❖ Mini lifesavers (boat theme)
- ❖ Sunglasses with inscribed lenses (lake theme)
- ❖ Suntan lotion (pool party theme)
- ❖ Microwave popcorn (movie theater theme)
- ❖ Ride ticket (carnival theme)
- ❖ Inscribed candy apple (carnival theme)
- ❖ Mini cowboy hat or boot (country western theme)
- ❖ Inscribed eye patch (pirate theme)
- ❖ Inscribed box of sparklers (Fourth of July theme)

❖ **Busy Bride** ❖ some of the save-the-date items above are for hand delivery only, such as the message in a bottle or bottle of green beer. So keep that in mind when you're making your decision.

If you're planning a destination wedding, you should mail your save-the-dates twelve months or more before the wedding date. This will give your guests time to save for the airfare and hotel costs. Also, this will give them time to request off from work, and allow them to book all their travel arrangements early enough. If you're planning a wedding in your hometown and your guest list . doesn't consist of many out-of-town guests, then you should mail your save-the-dates between nine and twelve months before the wedding date.

Fifteen

Wedding Rings

Your wedding rings are a symbol of your love and you will wear them every day for the rest of your lives. So take your time and shop around before you select your wedding rings. .

Some men decide to purchase the wedding rings solely on their own. I don't recommend this. Busy Bride, in today's world it is perfectly acceptable to accompany your fiancé when he goes shopping for wedding rings. Generally it is often easier for women to choose wedding rings, because women are often more familiar with jewelry than men. Most women already have an idea of the type of ring they want. Always keep in mind the four Cs: clarity, cut, color, and carat.

❖ **Busy Bride** ❖ stop. Remember, your wedding rings symbolize marriage and a couple's fidelity to one another when worn. Some brides even engrave "Do Not Remove" on the inside of their spouse's wedding band.

Here are some tips to use when purchasing wedding rings:

- ❖ Buy from a trusted jeweler.
- ❖ Establish a budget before you start shopping.
- ❖ Ask about the wedding bands and diamond warranty.
- ❖ Don't feel you have to purchase a wedding band that matches your groom's.

Today's busy brides are choosing platinum as their number one choice of wedding ring metal. Platinum is the hardest metal on the market today. If you love platinum, but can't afford the price tag, another option is white gold. It visibly looks like platinum, but it won't crush your budget.

Another modern trend is to incorporate diamonds into your groom's wedding band. Don't let your groom go overboard with diamonds too large or too many. It makes the ring look tacky and artificial.

The cost is what I consider the fifth C. Generally, the higher the cost, the better the cut, clarity, color, and carat. Most grooms spend two to three months' salary on their bride's engagement ring. This doesn't include the wedding bands. The wedding bands are additional costs the bride and groom pay for later. So the higher your groom's salary, the higher purchasing power for the engagement ring. For many men, the bride's engagement ring is considered a symbol of his prestige.

Sixteen

Bridal Gown
And Accessories

The bridal gown, or dress, is worn by the bride at her wedding ceremony. The bride's choice for the color and style of the bridal gown depends on her body type, wedding theme, formality, time of the wedding, location, color palette, culture, and religion. For example, years ago in China, brides wore a red bridal gown for good luck. Today, more and more brides in China are wearing white. The traditional bridal gown color in the United States is white, but more and more brides are wearing ivory, eggshell, and ecru. I recommend choosing a color and style that makes you feel fabulously beautiful, because it is your day to glow.

Don't forget to think about your body type. Do you have a small or large chest? What assets about your body would you like to accentuate in your bridal gown, and what body area would you like to hide? For example, if you have a tattoo you want to hide on your back, you should choose a bridal gown with a high-cut back to cover up the area. A low-cut or backless dress will not work.

❖ Busy Bride ❖ keep in mind that you want to make your groom's heart stop when he sees you in your bridal gown; you don't want your heart to stop when your bridal gown doesn't arrive in time because you ordered it too late. So don't start shopping too late. Between nine months to one year before the wedding, you should shop for your bridal gown. Order your bridal gown no later than six months before the wedding day. This will help to avoid the extra stress and extra charge to rush your bridal gown order. When ordering your bridal gown size, you should know it's easier for alterations if you order a size down from your normal dress size and have the bridal gown let out. Bridal gowns generally have a half to one inch of extra fabric on the sides of the gown that can easily be let out by a seamstress. If you order your bridal gown too big and have it taken in, you also have to take in the extra beading, cutwork, and fabric. This may alter the whole style of the bridal gown.

The five most popular and basic bridal gown styles are A-line/princess, mermaid or fishtail, ball gown, column, and empire. A successful bridal gown style is one that fits your body fabulously. Some bridal gown styles have different necklines, dress lengths, sleeve lengths, no sleeves, back lengths, no back, and the list goes on and on. Below is a list with detailed descriptions of the five basic bridal gown styles:

An A-line/princess bridal gown is fitted at the top and flares out wider toward the bottom. This style gown is cut to form a letter A form. This is a fabulous style for accentuating a bottom heavy figure.

A mermaid or fishtail bridal gown fits tight through the bodice and down through the hips. At the mid to lower calf area the gown flares out. This style can be difficult to wear for some body types. This is a fabulous style for an athletic or skinny figure because it adds curves.

A ball gown, or Cinderella bridal gown, is fitted at the top with a full skirt reaching to the floor on the bottom. This is a fabulous style for a taller or larger body type because it visually cuts the body in half and hides the tummy, hips, and legs.

A column bridal gown is a slender fitting dress with a very straight narrow-shaped cut, flowing from the top area straight to the floor. This is a fabulous style for a skinny petite figure because the cut helps elongate the body to create a taller appearance.

An empire bridal gown is known for its waistline that hits just below the bust line, or top portion of the waist, and then flows down to the floor or beyond. This is a fabulous style for a variety of body types from skinny to voluptuous as it adds curves while hiding the tummy, hips, and legs creating an overall long lean look.

Before you spend thousands on a bridal gown, I recommend taking a second to think about how long you will be in the gown and what you will be doing. At most weddings, the bride is in her bridal gown for ten or more hours, unless you purchase a second bridal gown for the reception. You will need to be able to walk, dance, sit, pose for pictures, use the restroom, and more, all in your bridal gown. So make sure you can move and that you're comfortable in the bridal gown before you make a final decision.

On average, most brides spend around nine hundred dollars on a bridal gown. The cost of your groom's attire and your bridal attire should be no more than ten percent of your total wedding budget. So keep your budget in mind when choosing your bridal gown, or at least get your dad's credit card and approval to splurge on that five thousand dollar or ten thousand dollar designer bridal gown!

Busy Bride, remember, it's your day and not your mom's, grandmother's, aunt's, or soon to be mother-in-law's day, so choose a fabulous gown that represents your style and wedding theme. Enjoy your shopping experience with your family and friends, because it is a once in a lifetime experience to be cherished forever.

Don't stress if you don't find the perfect dress right away. Take your time shopping and make the correct choice. Some brides try on fifty or more gowns before they find the perfect one. I recommend trying on at least ten to fifteen gowns before you make a final decision. Keep in mind that you will never know what you look like in a certain style gown if you don't try it on. So try, try, try, and try . . .

❖ Busy Bride ❖ stop. You can save money by shopping wedding designers' sample sales. You can go to your favorite designers' websites or e-mail them to ask when and where they will be holding sample sales events. This is an excellent way to buy a designer gown for half, or more, off the price.

Seventeen

Wedding Itinerary

Busy Bride, take the time to write a wedding itinerary, this will ensure that your wedding day runs smoothly. Of course unexpected events will occur, but if you have a wedding itinerary, the unexpected events are only small bumps because your wedding itinerary will keep you on track.

Couples who choose not to have a wedding itinerary experience unnecessary stress as more than half of their wedding day will not go as planned, because there is no plan or only the bride knows the plan.

For today's fabulous weddings, it's not enough to let everyone know what time the ceremony and reception start. You must write it all down, and you must plan and organize your day with as much attention to every detail as possible. Also, all your vendors will need a copy of your wedding itinerary too, so they will know the plan for the day as well.

Begin your itinerary with the rehearsal and rehearsal dinner, then from the moment you awake on your wedding day until the end of the reception. To guarantee your day runs smoothly, and you don't worry about every little detail, your wedding itinerary will serve as your Xanax.

❖ 𝕭usy 𝕭ride ❖ stop. Your work is done. Below is a sample wedding itinerary for you to use to plan your fabulous event. Just change the days and times to fit with your own timeline.

Friday
Wedding Ceremony Rehearsal
4:00 PM— Arrive at ceremony site
- ❖ Review additional ceremony items with ceremony site staff

5:00–6:00 PM—Rehearsal at ceremony site

6:30 PM— Rehearsal dinner

Saturday
Wedding Ceremony and Reception
10:00 AM—Awake and eat breakfast

11:00 AM—Shower and prepare for the day

Noon—Leave for hair appointment

1:00 PM—Hair appointment

3:30 PM—Wedding party arrives at ceremony site
- ❖ Distribute and pin all corsages and boutonnieres
- ❖ Photographer arrives

4:15 PM—Guests start arriving
- ❖ Ushers seat guests and distribute ceremony programs

4:30 PM—Wedding party enters
- ❖ Ceremony performed by wedding officiant

5:00 PM—Bride and groom's grand exit
- ❖ Wedding party exit
- ❖ Receiving line

5:15 PM—Bride and groom exit through white arch (with rice thrown by guests)
- ❖ Bride and groom enter horse carriage, or other type of vehicle, for ride
- ❖ Bar opens
- ❖ Guests invited into reception site for cocktails

5:30 PM—Wedding party photographs in garden area
- ❖ Dinner reception setting up in outside tent
- ❖ DJ setting up

6:00 PM—DJ begins while guests mingle inside and outside garden area
- ❖ Wedding party enters area outside reception tent and waits for grand entrance

6:30 PM—Guests are invited to enter reception tent and be seated for reception dinner

6:45 PM—Grand entrance of wedding party (announced by DJ)

6:55 PM—Toasts given by maid of honor, best man, bride, and groom

7:00 PM—Blessing of the food

7:05 PM—Dinner begins

8:00 PM—First dance

❖ Father-daughter dance

❖ Mother-son dance

❖ Bridal party dance

8:30 PM—Cake cutting under the white garden arch

❖ After cake cutting the photographer leaves

9:00–11:30 PM—Dancing and drinking

11:00 PM—Bar closes

11:15 PM—Last dance

11:30 PM—DJ leaves

❖ All wedding party and guests leave reception site

❖ Pack up of all wedding items

Remember, whatever happens, it is your day, so enjoy it!

❖ 𝕭usy 𝕭ride ❖ stop. Check your wedding itinerary. Your cocktail hour, or time between your ceremony and your reception, should be no longer than one hour, hence the name "cocktail hour." If your wedding itinerary schedules it for longer, change it. You don't want your guests getting bored or restless, or going home, before the reception starts.

Eighteen

Reception Caterer

F inding a catering company that cares about quality, quantity, and customer service is essential when planning a wedding. Your wedding guests are expecting a delicious feast, so don't let them down.

❖ **Busy Bride** ❖ keep in mind the one detail that everyone always remembers at a wedding—the food. If the food was terrible or if it was outstanding, your guests will remember.

The two types of wedding catering services are on-premise caterers and off-premise caterers. An on-premise catering service is one that prepares, cooks, and serves all the food at the same venue. Good examples of this type are a banquet hall or a country club. An off-premise catering service is one where the caterer prepares and cooks all the food in one location and then transports the food to the venue to be served. Good examples of this type are an aquarium, museum, or fire hall. These venues don't offer on-premise catering services, so you will have to choose an off-premise catering company to bring in and serve the prepared food.

When planning the wedding reception menu, you must keep in mind your budget, what you and your groom like to eat, and also what your families and friends like to eat. Remember—your wedding reception site, food, rentals, drinks, and cake should cost no more than fifty percent of your total wedding budget. So you will need to determine how much you can spend on each person, or your cpp (cost per person). Knowing your cpp will help when working with the catering company.

Next, consider the time of day your wedding reception will take place. Whether it's in the morning, afternoon, or evening, you will need to serve different options depending on the time. Most wedding receptions take place in the afternoon or evening.

The type of food service is also something to review with your caterer. Does the caterer provide buffet service, table service, or hors d'oeuvre service? If yes, how much does each cost? I recommend reviewing all your options and then choosing the best food service option for your wedding budget, theme, formality, time of day, and the food you want served.

❖ Busy Bride ❖ stop. If your catering company tries to persuade you to use family-style, or Russian-style, food service, don't allow it. Family-style, or Russian-style, food service is where platters of food are brought to the table and guests pass the platters around. I do not recommend this food service method. I believe it is tacky and distasteful. Don't make your guests share food with their table.

The next step is to decide on the menu. Below are some example menus for you to look at.

Example One   Breakfast Buffet

Pre-set table items—fresh fruit bowls, baskets of pastries, muffins, and bread, and a separate butter and jelly basket

Carving stations—　honey-baked ham
　　　　　　　　　　　roasted round beef
　　　　　　　　　　　roasted turkey breast

Omelet station—　　create your own omelet
Waffle station—　　create your own waffle
Buffet side dishes—　sausage patties
　　　　　　　　　　　buttermilk pancakes
　　　　　　　　　　　smoked salmon
　　　　　　　　　　　cold cereals
　　　　　　　　　　　scrambled eggs
　　　　　　　　　　　bacon
　　　　　　　　　　　French toast
　　　　　　　　　　　hash browns with cheese
　　　　　　　　　　　potato casserole
　　　　　　　　　　　sliced ham

grits

oatmeal

Beverages—juice, coffee, tea, water, champagne, and your signature wedding cocktail

Dessert—wedding cake, of course, and any additional favorite desserts

Example Two   Seated or Sit-down Breakfast

Pre-set table items—fresh fruit bowls, baskets of pastries, muffins, and bread, and a separate butter and jelly basket

Served meals (have your guests choose one)—

* ❖ *Veggie-cheese omelet* with toast, ham, hash browns, oatmeal, and strawberry or blueberry parfait
* ❖ *Buttermilk pancakes* with ham, bacon, sausage, hash browns, eggs, and toast
* ❖ *French toast* with ham, bacon, sausage, hash browns, eggs, and toast
* ❖ *Belgian waffles* with ham, bacon, sausage, hash browns, eggs, and toast

Beverages—juice, coffee, tea, water, champagne, and your signature wedding cocktail

Dessert—wedding cake and any additional favorite desserts

❖ **Busy Bride** ❖ stop. Know that you can always add some other favorite desserts for your guests to enjoy in addition to your wedding cake. I recommend Italian cookies, tiramisu, New York style cheesecake, chocolate mousse, and key lime tarts. These are all fabulous dessert options to include with your wedding cake. Keep in mind to choose additional desserts that you and your groom enjoy, and that also coordinate with your wedding formality, theme, and menu.

Example Three   Lunch Buffet

Hors d'oeuvres—open-faced finger sandwiches
coconut shrimp with marmalade sauce
fresh fruit with dip
cheese, pepperoni, and crackers
fresh vegetables with dip
crabmeat with cocktail sauce
smoked salmon with capers, red onions, lemon, and wafers
Pre-set table items—hot dinner rolls with butter and a tossed garden salad
Carving stations—honey-baked ham
roasted round beef
roasted turkey breast

Pasta station—with meatballs, ziti, angel hair
pasta, marinara, and Alfredo sauces

Buffet side dishes—cold pasta salad
fresh fruit salad
coleslaw
three-bean salad
roasted vegetables
baked potato
macaroni and cheese
broccoli rice au gratin
sweet potato casserole
glazed carrots
Italian wedding soup
clam chowder
chicken noodle soup

Beverages—coffee, tea, water, sodas, nonalcoholic
punch, beer, wine, champagne, mixed drinks,
and your signature wedding cocktail

Dessert—again, your wedding cake and any
additional favorite desserts

Example Four   Seated or Sit-down Lunch

Hors d'oeuvres (served on silver trays to each
guest)—
mini crab cakes
scallops wrapped in bacon
bruschetta
mini quiche
breaded oysters

lobster bisque

Pre-set table items—hot dinner rolls with butter and a tossed garden salad

Served meals (have your guests choose one)—

- ❖ *Roasted chicken breast* with baked potato and vegetable medley
- ❖ *Grilled salmon* with baked potato and vegetable medley
- ❖ *Vegetarian lasagna* with green beans and almonds and vegetable medley
- ❖ *Prime rib of beef* with horseradish, baked potato, and vegetable medley

Beverages—coffee, tea, water, sodas, nonalcoholic punch, beer, wine, champagne, mixed drinks, and your signature wedding cocktail

Dessert—wedding cake and any additional favorite desserts

Example Five Dinner Buffet

Hors d'oeuvres—fresh fruit with chocolate dipping sauce

fresh vegetables with
dipping sauce
cheese, pepperoni, and
crackers
fried calamari
stuffed mushrooms
franks in a blanket

scallops wrapped in bacon

Pre-set table items—fresh-baked sweet dinner rolls with butter and a tossed garden salad

Carving stations—roasted prime rib of beef
roasted pork loin
honey-glazed ham
roasted turkey breast

Additional food stations (choose 2-3 food stations from below)—

* *Fajita station* has sizzling chicken and beef fajitas prepared to order. Toppings include salsa, sour cream, guacamole, peppers, shredded cheese, lettuce, onions, and refried beans

* *Italian station* prepared to order items include tripe in marinara sauce over linguini, eggplant parmesan in marinara over linguini, and shrimp and scallops in marinara or Alfredo over linguini

* *Pasta station* has prepared to order pasta with any of the below ingredients: *Pastas* choices are ziti, angel hair, bow tie, and cheese tortellini. *Sauces* are marinara, vodka sauce, and Alfredo sauce. *Additional Ingredients* include broccoli, garlic, olive oil, mushrooms, peppers, caramelized onions, green scallions, beef, and sausage

❖ ***Stir-fry station*** includes sautéed chicken, pork, seafood, and beef. Served with oriental vegetables, stir-fried rice, steamed rice, and vegetable spring rolls

❖ ***Sushi station*** includes seafood and vegetable sushi (like California, spicy tuna, shrimp, and salmon). All prepared to order with soy sauce, wasabi, and pickled ginger

❖ ***Seafood station*** has fresh oysters shucked to order, smoked salmon, jumbo shrimp, crab claws, and cocktail sauce

❖ ***Soup station*** offers Italian wedding soup, chicken noodle soup, vegetable soup, and French onion soup

❖ ***Mashed or baked potato station*** has mashed potatoes prepared to order. Toppings include bacon, cheddar cheese, sour cream, chives, mushrooms, broccoli, and gravy

Buffet side dishes—fresh tomatoes and mozzarella in olive oil

seasoned roasted vegetables
bourbon-glazed carrots
roasted red potatoes
sweet potato casserole
creamed corn

fresh asparagus tips with
hollandaise sauce
fried okra
risotto
collard greens

Beverages—coffee, tea, water, sodas, nonalcoholic
punch, beer, wine, champagne, mixed drinks,
and your signature wedding cocktail

Dessert—wedding cake and any additional favorite
desserts

Example Six   Seated or Sit-down Dinner

Cold hors d'oeuvres (served on silver trays to each
guest)—
fresh shrimp with cocktail
sauce
fresh raw oysters on the half
shell with crackers, lemon,
and cocktail sauce
melon wrapped in prosciutto
baguette

Hot hors d'oeuvres (served on silver trays to each
guest)—
mini beef Wellingtons
clams casino
shrimp scampi
quiche lorraine

assorted filled puff pastries
fried calamari
Swedish meatballs
mini chicken cordon bleu

Pre-set table items—fresh-baked sweet dinner rolls with butter and a tossed garden or Mediterranean salad

Soups (have your guests choose one)—

minestrone
cream of broccoli
seafood bisque
Italian wedding soup

Served meals (have your guests choose one)—

* ❖ *Filet mignon* with glazed carrots, twice-baked potatoes, and green beans with almonds and garlic
* ❖ *Rack of lamb* with glazed carrots, twice-baked potatoes, and green beans with almonds and garlic
* ❖ *Lobster tail* with glazed carrots, twice-baked potatoes, and green beans with almonds and garlic
* ❖ *Brasciole*, or seasoned steak, with ground beef mixture, cappicola, and a hard-boiled egg in the middle. Served over linguini
* ❖ *Chicken cordon bleu* with glazed carrots, twice-baked potatoes, and green beans with almonds and garlic

❖ *Stuffed flounder* with glazed carrots, twice-baked potatoes, and green beans with almonds and garlic

Beverages—coffee, tea, water, sodas, nonalcoholic punch, beer, wine, champagne, mixed drinks, and your signature wedding cocktail

Dessert—wedding cake and any additional favorite desserts

Example Seven Hors D'oeuvres Buffet or Cocktail Reception

Hors d'oeuvres—finger sandwiches
chicken fingers
fried raviolis
chicken wings
mozzarella sticks
crab puffs
fresh fruit and cheeses
Swedish meatballs
stuffed mushrooms
fresh vegetables with dip
fried zucchini

Beverages—coffee, tea, water, sodas, nonalcoholic punch, beer, wine, champagne, mixed drinks, and your signature wedding cocktail

Dessert—wedding cake and any additional favorite desserts

These examples are meant to help you decide on your wedding menu. You can use parts of each menu example above or just totally copy one menu example. Some brides get really creative with their menu options and add fondue pots, fountains, and even food stations from around the world. Whatever your style is, don't forget to incorporate your wedding formality, theme, color palette, and budget boundaries.

❖ **Busy Bride** ❖ stop. Read these "dos" and "don'ts" for selecting a wedding caterer:

- ❖ Do ask for a copy of the catering company's business license, most recent health department rating, and liability insurance. Make sure the insurance policy gives at least one million dollars or more in coverage.
- ❖ Do ask for a contract with your catering company. This guarantees, in writing, that the company will provide the services agreed upon.
- ❖ Do make sure you can taste your menu selection.
- ❖ Do ask about any additional costs. For example, taxes, additional fees, and gratuities.
- ❖ Don't forget to ask if the catering company can provide chairs, tables, equipment, linens, dinnerware, glassware, silverware, wait staff, bartenders, wedding cake, alcohol, bar services, valet services, lighting, or any other

wedding elements you might need. By utilizing the caterer for other services too, you can usually receive a package deal, or at least a discount, on the add-on services.

❖ Don't forget to receive a receipt for any deposits and payments for your records as proof of payment.

❖ *Busy Bride* ❖ stop. Keep in mind that, for your guests, your food and drinks will be some of the most important elements at your wedding reception. So make sure your guests are well fed and have a few great cocktails, so they are sure to have a fabulous time.

Beverages

The traditional golden standard for most weddings is an open bar for guests to enjoy, giving your guests the ultimate opportunity to drink on someone else's dime.

Today, brides and grooms have several different beverage options to choose from.

❖ *Busy Bride* ❖ below is a list of the common wedding beverage options:

❖ Full open bar

- ❖ Cash bar
- ❖ Beer and wine only bar
- ❖ Nonalcoholic bar

The type of beverage option you choose should be based on your budget, personal taste, and religious beliefs as a couple. Also, it is thoughtful to consider your guests' preferences as well as your own.

❖ **Busy Bride** ❖ stop. Remember, your wedding beverage budget is included in your reception budget, which is fifty percent of the total wedding budget. So grab a calculator and do the math.

After you have decided on your wedding beverage option, the next step is to check with your reception site, or venue, and see what types of beverage services they provide.

❖ **Busy Bride** ❖ stop. You need to find out what the local laws are that regulate the serving of alcoholic beverages. In most areas, the party serving alcoholic beverages must have a liquor license. Most banquet halls and catering companies already have a license, but stop and get a copy of their liquor license and make sure your bar is legal. If you are running your own bar, you may be required to obtain a one-day special liquor license from the government authority that regulates bars and taverns in your area.

While your reception is a celebration of your wedding, alcohol is not always a necessity for the celebration. If you decide on a nonalcoholic bar, there are many creative alternatives. For example, you could have a nonalcoholic juice or smoothie bar, and a nonalcoholic toast with sparkling cider or grape juice in place of champagne.

If your reception site, or venue, will not be providing beverage services, then you will need to hire an outside beverage service company and purchase the beverages and bar essentials. Below is a list of beverages and bar essentials to help you when you're stocking your bar.

Beverages
- ❖ Champagne
- ❖ Light beer
- ❖ Regular beer
- ❖ White wine
- ❖ Red wine
- ❖ Vodka
- ❖ Gin
- ❖ Light rum
- ❖ Dark rum

- ❖ Tequila
- ❖ Whiskey
- ❖ Scotch
- ❖ Bourbon
- ❖ Dry vermouth
- ❖ Sweet vermouth
- ❖ Irish cream
- ❖ Amaretto
- ❖ Southern Comfort
- ❖ Brandy
- ❖ Cognac

Additional Nonessential Liqueurs

- ❖ Triple sec
- ❖ Various flavors of schnapps
- ❖ Kahlúa
- ❖ Crème de menthe
- ❖ Cointreau
- ❖ Blue curaçao
- ❖ Tia Maria
- ❖ Sambuca
- ❖ Chambord
- ❖ Crème de banana
- ❖ Godiva
- ❖ Midori
- ❖ Rumple Minze
- ❖ Jägermeister
- ❖ Goldschläger
- ❖ Galliano

- Frangelico
- Crème de cacao
- Grand Marnier

❖ 𝔅usy 𝔅ride ❖ stop. Don't forget to purchase all the ingredients for your signature wedding cocktail or cocktails.

Mixers

- Cola
- Diet cola
- Lemon-lime soda
- Ginger ale
- Tonic water
- Soda water
- Cranberry juice
- Grenadine
- Lime juice
- Fruit punch
- Margarita mix
- Pineapple juice
- Orange juice
- Grapefruit juice
- Tomato juice
- Lemonade
- Cream
- Milk
- Sour mix

❖ Bitters

Condiments
❖ Salt and pepper
❖ Worcestershire sauce
❖ Tabasco sauce
❖ Cherries
❖ Olives
❖ Lemons
❖ Limes
❖ Oranges
❖ Cocktail onions
❖ Strawberries
❖ Blueberries
❖ Watermelon
❖ Grapes
❖ Pineapple
❖ Bananas
❖ Nutmeg
❖ Whip cream

Bar Essentials
❖ Ice (one pound per person)
❖ Ice bucket
❖ Tongs
❖ Cocktail shakers
❖ Jiggers
❖ Cocktail strainers
❖ Spoons

❖ Stirrers
❖ Beverage cooler
❖ Wine bottle opener
❖ Glassware
❖ Bar condiment tray
❖ Straws
❖ Napkins
❖ Umbrellas
❖ Trash can
❖ Bar towel

❖ **Busy Bride** ❖ don't wait until the last minute to purchase your beverages and bar essentials. I recommend purchasing everything, except the perishables, at least a month or more ahead to ensure no last minute surprises.

❖ **Busy Bride** ❖ stop. Here's an easy tip to estimate how much alcohol your guests will drink. On average, each guest will drink one to two drinks an hour at a wedding. Your older guests might drink less, but your younger guests might drink more. So either way it balances out. Multiply the amount of hours the bar will be open by the number of guests attending by the number of drinks per hour (either one or two, also depends on the time of day and group of guests) that will equal a close estimation of how many drinks your guests will consume.

If your wedding venue provides a bar, you will need to ask about their bar packages. Ask your reception venue manager for a per guest per hour price for an open bar. On average, the price per guest per hour can be anywhere from five dollars to twenty dollars depending on the venue and alcohol. A top shelf stocked bar is going to be your most expensive price per guest per hour. A less expensive price per guest per hour is a non-name brand, or house brand, stocked bar.

❖ **Busy Bride** ❖ stop. Here's another beverage option, an open consumption bar. Check with your reception venue because only some reception venues offer this option. A consumption bar is one that tallies all drinks as your guests order them and are added to the final bill. With this option, you have full control over the bar and can cap the bar at a certain amount. This is a cheaper option for an open-bar reception, where the average guest doesn't consume that much alcohol.

The number one way to save money on a wedding bar package is to close the bar during the meal. Now this is only a money saving option for a buffet or sit-down reception, because your guests are occupied eating. For cocktail or hors d'oeuvre receptions, this is not an option. But think of it this way, you're already saving on the meal.

The last wedding beverage money saving tip is to ask about the fees. Ask if there is a fee for setup, corkage, bartender gratuity, and open unfinished bottles of alcohol. Whatever wedding beverage option you choose, get it in writing before the event. Then after the event, ask for a complete consumption report. Busy Bride, you need to watch out for scams, so you don't get financially taken advantage of by your wedding vendors.

Nineteen

Ceremony Music

O n the biggest day of your life let your wedding ceremony music enhance your cherished moments and create fabulous wedding memories. Keep in mind that your ceremony music will help the ceremony flow from the vows to the unity candle, or ritual, all the way through the recessional. Music brings together all the visual and oral elements to create a memorable event.

The seven standard segments of most wedding ceremonies are as follows: the ceremony prelude, the ceremony wedding party processional, the ceremony bridal processional, the ceremony interlude, the ceremony unity candle lighting or other ritual, the ceremony recessional, and the ceremony postlude. Below I go into greater detail on each segment and list my favorite music selections for each.

Ceremony Prelude

The prelude music will typically be played prior to the start of the ceremony while guests are being seated. Generally, five or six songs are played as prelude music. Keep in mind that the songs set the tone for the entire ceremony.

❖ 𝕭𝖚𝖘𝖞 𝕭𝖗𝖎𝖉𝖊 ❖ stop here. Your work is done. Below is a list of glorious songs that you may want to use as prelude music:

- ❖ "So This Is Love" Instrumental from *Cinderella* by David, Hoffman, and Livingston
- ❖ "Ave Maria" by Schubert
- ❖ "As Time Goes By (A Kiss is Just a Kiss)" by Tony Bennett
- ❖ *The Four Seasons* by Vivaldi
- ❖ "Wind Beneath My Wings" by Bette Midler
- ❖ "Unchained Melody" by The Righteous Brothers
- ❖ "The Rose" by Bette Midler
- ❖ "Have I Told You Lately" by Rod Stewart
- ❖ *Water Music* by Handel
- ❖ Adagio from Sonata in E-flat by Mozart
- ❖ "Waltz" from *The Sleeping Beauty* ballet, op. 66, Act 1, scene 6 composed by Tchaikovsky, performed by the Philharmonia Orchestra of London

Ceremony Wedding Party Processional

The wedding party processional music symbolizes the official start of the ceremony. I recommend choosing music that's smooth and flowing like the sounds of water flowing down a river. While this music is playing, the bridesmaids and groomsmen are typically walking down the aisle, followed by the ring bearer, or bearers, and then the flower girl, or girls.

❖ 𝕭usy 𝕭ride ❖ stop here. Your work is done. Below is a list of fabulous songs that you may want to use as wedding party processional music:

- ❖ "Sheep May Safely Graze" by Johann Sebastian Bach
- ❖ Theme from the last movement of Symphony no. 9 by Beethoven
- ❖ Gavotte from Orchestral Suite no. 3 by Johann Sebastian Bach
- ❖ "Trumpet Tune" by Henry Purcell
- ❖ "Reflections of Passion" by Yanni
- ❖ "Saint Anthony's Chorale" by Johannes Brahms
- ❖ "Trumpet Voluntary (The Prince of Denmark's March)" by Jeremiah Clarke
- ❖ Canon in D by Johann Pachelbel
- ❖ "Jesu, Joy of Man's Desiring" by Johann Sebastian Bach

Ceremony Bridal Processional

The bridal processional, or bride's grand entrance, music starts after the entire wedding party has made it down the aisle. The bridal processional music will begin, the crowd will rise, and then the bride will enter and proceed down the aisle to the altar. Some brides walk alone or are escorted by their father, uncle, brother, or good friend. The bridal processional is one of the most glorious and memorable moments of the entire wedding day. I recommend taking your time choosing your favorite song, because you will remember the song and the moment for a lifetime.

❖ *Busy Bride* ❖ stop here. Your work is done. Below is a list of glorious songs that you may want to use as bridal processional music:

- ❖ "Here Comes the Bride" or "Bridal Chorus" or "Wedding March" from *Lohengrin* by Wagner
- ❖ "Rigaudon" by Andre Campra
- ❖ "Wedding March" by Tchaikovsky
- ❖ Canon in D by Johann Pachelbel
- ❖ "Trumpet Voluntary (The Prince of Demark's March)" by Jeremiah Clarke
- ❖ "Chapel of Love" by Dixie Cups
- ❖ "Somewhere Over the Rainbow" by Doris Day

Ceremony Interlude

The ceremony interlude music is played anytime in the ceremony when there are no words being spoken and no activity for at least a minute. Interlude music is a great way to adjust the pace of the ceremony, or add focus to a special moment in the ceremony. Three or four interlude songs can fill in the silent spaces and give your ceremony a wonderful flow.

❖ Busy Bride ❖ stop here. Your work is done. Below is a list of fabulous songs you may want to use as interlude music:

- ❖ "Endless Love" by Lionel Richie and Diana Ross
- ❖ Arioso in A by Johann Sebastian Bach
- ❖ "Clair de Lune" by Claude Debussy
- ❖ "A Moment Like This" by Kelly Clarkson
- ❖ "Amazed" by Lonestar
- ❖ "The Lord's Prayer" by Malotte
- ❖ "Truly Madly Deeply" by Savage Garden
- ❖ "You Raise Me Up" by Josh Groban
- ❖ "We've Only Just Begun" by The Carpenters
- ❖ "The Wedding Song" by Noel Paul Stookey
- ❖ "Once Upon A Time . . . Storybook Love" from *The Princess Bride* by Mark Knopfler
- ❖ "Annie's Song" by John Denver
- ❖ "Speak Softly Love" from *The Godfather* by Al Martino from
- ❖ "Thank You" by Led Zeppelin

❖ **Busy Bride** ❖ stop. Remember to choose three or four ceremony interlude songs so your guests won't have to hear the same song over and over throughout the wedding ceremony.

Ceremony Unity Candle or Other Ritual

The most popular type of wedding ceremony ritual is the unity candle. There are many other rituals such as a rose ceremony, other flower ritual, sand, stones, crystals, wine ritual, and many more. All these ceremony rituals are generally accompanied by music. When choosing music for your ceremony ritual, keep in mind that the music should not take away from, or distract your guests away from, the ceremony ritual. The music should be used to enhance the special unity and help explain the symbolism of the unity candle or other ritual preformed.

❖ **Busy Bride** ❖ stop here. Your work is done. Below is a list of glorious songs that you may want to use as unity candle or other ritual music:

- ❖ "The Wedding Song" by Kenny G
- ❖ "Love Theme from St. Elmo's Fire (Just for a Moment)" by David Foster
- ❖ "Circle of Life" by Elton John
- ❖ "Forever and For Always" by Shania Twain

- ❖ "All My Life" by K-Ci and JoJo
- ❖ "What a Wonderful World" by Louis Armstrong
- ❖ "This Little Light of Mine" by Elizabeth Mitchell
- ❖ "Two Flames That Glow" by Elaine McDonald and David Gerard
- ❖ "You Light Up My Life" by Debby Boone
- ❖ "Ode to Joy" from Symphony no. 9 by Beethoven
- ❖ "Dreamgift" by Brewer

❖ Ꝙusy Ꝙride ❖ stop. You can save money by listening to most of these songs on YouTube where you can listen to songs for free.

Ceremony Recessional

The ceremony recessional music starts after the wedding officiant pronounces you husband and wife. Generally everyone claps and then the ceremony recessional music begins. I recommend choosing a song that is bright, joyous, upbeat, and full of celebration.

Some couples choose a favorite song from a movie or hobby. Keep in mind that your song starts the beginning of your celebration as newlyweds and should get your guests revved up for the reception to follow. The ceremony recessional music is played as the entire wedding party leaves and may still be playing as the guests start to be escorted out.

❖ Busy Bride ❖ stop here. Your work is done. Below is a list of fabulous songs that you may want to use as recessional music:

- ❖ "Rondeau" by Jean-Joseph Mouret
- ❖ "Wedding March" from *A Midsummer Night's Dream* by Felix Mendelssohn
- ❖ "Happy Together" by The Turtles
- ❖ "Pomp and Circumstance" by Elgar
- ❖ "At Last" by Etta James
- ❖ "Celebration" by Kool and the Gang
- ❖ "From This Moment On" by Shania Twain featuring the Backstreet Boys
- ❖ "Walking on Sunshine" by Katrina and the Waves
- ❖ "You Are the Sunshine Of My Life" by Stevie Wonder
- ❖ "What a Wonderful World" by Louis Armstrong
- ❖ "La Rejouissance" by Handel

Ceremony Postlude

The ceremony postlude music is played after the ceremony recessional music. The music played should set a fabulous and delightful tone as guests exit the ceremony site. If you choose to have a receiving line, then the music you choose for the ceremony postlude will play until all your guests exit the ceremony site and receiving line.

❖ Busy Bride ❖ stop here. Your work is done. Below is a list of glorious songs that you may want to use as postlude music:

- ❖ "Autumn" from *The Four Seasons* by Vivaldi
- ❖ "I'll Always Love You" by Taylor Dayne
- ❖ "Quando me'n vò (Musette's Waltz)" from *La Bohème* by Giacomo Puccini
- ❖ "Angels" by Robin Thicke
- ❖ "Joyful, Joyful, We Adore Thee" composed by Beethoven with words by Henry Van Dyke
- ❖ "With You" by Chris Brown

In conclusion, Busy Bride, have fun and enjoy the process of choosing your wedding ceremony music. Music is a form of expression so take advantage and utilize the music to express your feelings, your style, and the theme of your wedding.

Twenty

Reception Music

Years from now, you and your wedding guests will only remember a handful of details from your reception. Your guests will certainly remember if they danced, laughed, and enjoyed themselves. So when choosing your reception music, keep in mind that the entertainment factor will make or break your reception. Your wedding reception music will set the tone for the entire reception event. So, think about the mood you want to create and the atmosphere, or reception site, you have to create it in.

Next, you must decide whether or not there will be dancing at your reception. Also, you must decide if you would like a live band, DJ, or both to provide the music for the reception. While live bands are generally more expensive, live music is often viewed as being more fabulously upscale than a DJ service. If budget is the main issue, a DJ service is definitely the more cost effective music entertainment choice. Whichever one you choose, remember that you need to see the entertainers in action before you commit. This will give you a taste of how they dress, their entertainment style, music quality, and how they work the crowd. These are all essential elements that a fabulous wedding entertainer must possess.

❖ **Busy Bride** ❖ keep in mind that your reception and ceremony music should be no more than seven percent of your total wedding budget. So Busy Bride, get your calculator and do the math, or call your dad and ask for more money.

❖ **Busy Bride** ❖ stop. Your work is done. Below are all your interview questions for your entertainer. So setup your interview appointments and ask away.

1. Is the entertainer available on the date of your wedding?
2. How long has the entertainer been in business?
3. How many weddings has the entertainer entertained at your reception site?
4. How many weddings does the entertainer entertain each year?
5. What type of equipment and music selections does the entertainer have?
6. Ask to see a video of one of the entertainer's wedding performances.
7. Ask if you can attend one of the entertainer's upcoming performances.

8. Does the entertainer have a backup entertainer in case of an emergency?
9. Does the entertainer have backup equipment in case of an emergency?
10. Ask if the entertainer provides additional services, like lighting.
11. Ask if the entertainer has three or more brides you can contact as references. If an entertainer can't provide three or more recent satisfied brides or customers, you need to pass on that entertainer before you become another one of his or her unsatisfied brides.
12. Ask for a package price list.
13. Ask if the packages include setup and breakdown time.
14. Ask about additional costs.
15. Ask about overtime costs.
16. Ask about the first deposit amount and schedule of payments.
17. Does the entertainer have a cancellation policy or refund policy?
18. Does the entertainer carry liability insurance?
19. Does the entertainer provide a written contract?
20. What kind of space or stage does the entertainer require?
21. Can the entertainer play specific requests?
22. Can the entertainer play a "must play" list provided by you?

Your wedding entertainment will be one of the biggest reasons for success or failure at your wedding reception. So make sure you ask the questions above and get the answers that fit your personal wedding style and theme.

Every wedding reception has a personality, and a skilled DJ or bandleader will be able to adapt to your wedding reception personality. He or she will be able to play songs and music at the correct times to create a great party, while also incorporating your "must play" list and additional song requests from your guests.

After meeting with three or more entertainers and asking them the interview questions I provided above, you should know which entertainer you want to commit to. The next step is to review the entertainer's written contract and check for all the essential elements.

❖ Busy Bride ❖ below is a checklist of all the essential elements that should be found in your written contract with the wedding entertainer:

1. The entertainer's name, address, and phone numbers (the company's information and all the actual entertainer information)

2. Your name (Busy Bride), address, and phone numbers

3. Your groom's name, address, and phone numbers

4. The address of your reception site, the dates, and the times that the entertainers will arrive and depart

5. The name and contact information for the emergency, or backup, entertainer

6. The names of all entertainers

7. All services provided related to the entertainment package purchased

8. Schedule of fees

9. Any additional costs

10. Hours of service

11. Overtime rates

12. Entertainer's setup requirements

13. Entertainer's attire

14. Breaks and meal requirements

15. Detailed information for alternative plans, in case of bad weather

16. Deposit policy

17. Date of the first deposit, amount of the first deposit, and amount still owed

18. Cancellation policy

19. Entertainer's liability insurance policy

20. Any guarantees

21. Your signatures (Busy Bride and Groom) and the date, and the entertainment's signature(s) and the date

After the written entertainer's contract successfully passes the essential elements test, you, your groom, and the entertainer may sign and date the contract. I recommend signing two copies of the contract, one for your records and one for the entertainer's records. Now take a deep breath and relax. As long as you followed all my advice from above, you have made an intelligent decision.

❖ **Busy Bride** ❖ stop. Keep in mind that the best wedding entertainers' schedules fill up fast, so book as early as possible. I recommend you start interviewing wedding entertainers at least nine to twelve months before your wedding, and book your wedding entertainer no later than nine months before the wedding.

❖ **Busy Bride** ❖ stop. Be prepared. Put together a list of names and the order to be announced at the grand entrance. Include all name pronunciations to help the entertainer properly announce all the wedding party attendants. Generally, the bride's grandparents enter first, followed by the groom's grandparents, the bride's parents, the groom's parents, the bridal party, and the bride and groom last.

Make your reception a fabulous night to be remembered. So whatever happens, just remember it is your time to celebrate. Enjoy your night and your guests will also enjoy it.

❖ Busy Bride ❖ the next step is to create your reception music "must play" list. Think about the atmosphere, tone, and style you want to create at your reception. These are all important factors when choosing your music. Don't forget to include your wedding theme, because everything must always coordinate. Below is a list of events held at most wedding receptions and some possible song selections. Each of these events should have a special song chosen to be played. Your wedding reception may have different events, depending on the theme, mood, and your personal style. All the songs you choose for your wedding are then compiled to create your "must play" list. This list is then given to your reception entertainers so they can follow it. Below are some example songs to help you create your "must play" list:

Cocktail Hour or Social Hour
"Margaritaville" by Jimmy Buffett
"New York, New York" by Frank Sinatra
"Chapel of Love" by The Dixie Cups
"That's Amore" by Dean Martin
"Time After Time" by Cyndi Lauper
"Turn Your Lights Down Low" by Bob Marley
"When a Man Loves a Woman" by Percy Sledge and Michael Bolton
"Summer of '69" by Bryan Adams

"I'm Gonna Be" by The Proclaimers
"Mambo Italiano" by Dean Martin

Wedding Party Grand Entrance
"Celebration" by Kool and the Gang
"Get Ready for This" by 2 Unlimited
"Party Like a Rockstar" by Shop Boyz
"Angelina/Zooma Zooma" by Louis Prima
"At Last" by Etta James

First Dance (for Bride and Groom)
"Can't Help Falling in Love" by Elvis Presley
"I Have But One Heart" by Al Martino
"Endless Love" by Lionel Richie and Diana Ross
"Wonderful Tonight" by Eric Clapton
"All My Life" by K-Ci and JoJo
"When a Man Loves a Woman" by Percy Sledge and Michael Bolton
"Unforgettable" by Nat King Cole
"The Wedding Song" by Noel Paul Stookey

Father-Daughter Dance
"A Song for My Daughter on Her Wedding Day" by Mikki Viereck
"Daddy's Little Girl" by Al Martino
"(You'll Always be) My Little Girl" by Steve Kirwan
"Butterfly Kisses" by Bob Carlisle
"My Little Girl" by Tim McGraw

Mother-Son Dance

"A Song for My Son on His Wedding Day" by Mikki Viereck

"Mama" by Jerry Vale

"A Song for My Mama" by Boyz II Men

"In Your Eyes" by David Chamberlin

"The Man You've Become" by Molly Pasutti

Bridal Party Dance

"Unchained Melody" from the *Ghost* soundtrack by North and Zaret

"Dancing Queen" by ABBA

"That's Amore" by Dean Martin

"That's What Friends are For" by Dionne Warwick with Elton John, Gladys Knight, and Stevie Wonder

Money or Dollar Dance

"If I had a Million Dollars" by Barenaked Ladies

"Money (That's What I Want)" by Flying Lizards

"For the Love of Money" by O'Jays

"Money, Money" from *Cabaret* by Kander and Ebb

Bouquet Toss

"It's Raining Men" by Weather Girls

"This One's for the Girls" by Martina McBride

"Girls Just Want to Have Fun" by Cyndi Lauper

"Another One Bites the Dust" by Queen

Garter Removal
"Stripper" by David Rose
"I'm Too Sexy" by Right Said Fred

Garter Toss
"Who Let the Dogs Out??" by Baha Men
"Pour Some Sugar on Me" by Def Leppard

Garter Placement
"Let's Get it On" by Marvin Gaye
"Hot in Here" by Nelly
"Sexual Healing" by Marvin Gaye

Cutting the Cake
"Hit Me with Your Best Shot" by Pat Benatar
"Happy Together" by The Turtles
"Love and Marriage" by Frank Sinatra
"Sugar, Sugar" by The Archies
"The Godfather" by Italian Violin

Last Dance
"From this Moment On" by Shania Twain featuring the Backstreet Boys
"I've Had the Time of My Life" by Bill Medley and Jennifer Warnes
"Good Riddance (Time of Your Life)" by Green Day
"Save the Last Dance for Me" by The Drifters
"Goodnight, Sweetheart, Goodnight" by the Spaniels
"Bunoa Sera" by Louis Prima

Additional "Must Play" Favorites

"December, 1963 (Oh, What a Night)" by the
Four Seasons
"Dancing Queen" by ABBA
"Lady in Red" by Chris de Burgh
Your favorite songs

"Must Play" Italian Favorites

"Eh Cumpari" from *The Godfather Part II* by
Julius La Rosa
"Angelina/Zooma Zooma" by Louis Prima
"Volare" by Dean Martin
"To Each His Own" from *The Godfather Part
III* sung by Al Martino
"That's Amore" by Dean Martin

Twenty-One

Photographer

C apture your fabulous wedding memories and treasure them forever through your wedding photography. Your wedding photographs are going to be the keepsakes you will cherish and save after the thousands of dollars and many hours you will spend on planning the most important day of your life—your wedding day. So don't take choosing a photographer lightly. If you do, you may regret it forever.

❖ *Busy Bride* ❖ choosing a wedding photographer is almost as important as choosing a spouse. I recommend interviewing at least three or more photographers. Keep in mind that once you have made your decision, there is no second chance at recapturing those wedding memories if you choose the wrong photographer.

The essential elements to keep in mind when choosing your perfect photographer are price, experience, chemistry, photographic style, and his or her references. Busy Bride, you need to remember that your wedding photographer or videographer or both should cost no more than ten percent of your total wedding budget. If you choose to use only a photographer, you will have more money to spend. If you choose to use both a photographer and a videographer, you must divide the budget in half.

❖ *Busy Bride* ❖ below is a list of interview questions to ask when you interview photographers:

1. How many years of experience does the photographer have?

2. What is the photographer's specialty (wedding, family portraits, etc.)?

3. What is the photographer's photographic style (traditional, photojournalistic, formal, candid, etc.)?

4. Does the photographer have formal training or a college education in photography?

5. How many weddings a year does the photographer photograph?

6. Will he or she be the photographer photographing your wedding?

7. Does the photographer have an assistant, or other staff member, who works with him or her?

8. Does the photographer have a replacement, or backup photographer, in case of an emergency?

9. What type of photography equipment does the photographer use?

10. Does the photographer have backup photography equipment? If yes, is it the same quality as the regular photography equipment?

11. Is the photographer's personality one that you can get along with?

12. Is the photographer within your budget?

13. On average, how many photographs does the photographer shoot at a typical wedding?

14. Will the photographer accept and shoot your "must photograph" list?

15. Has the photographer photographed at your ceremony or reception sites or both before?

16. How many hours will the photographer photograph at your wedding?
17. What types of packages does the photographer offer?
18. Are there any additional costs?
19. Ask to view the photographer's portfolio.
20. Ask to see samples of previous weddings the photographer has photographed.
21. Are the negatives, or a CD, of the photographs included in the package price?
22. When will the photographer have the negatives ready to be viewed?
23. When will the photographer have the prints and album complete?
24. Does the photographer have a website?
25. Can the photographer provide references?
26. Ask the photographer what he or she does with the negatives once your prints and album are complete.
27. If the photographer doesn't include negatives in his or her packages, can you purchase them?
28. Ask what type of lighting the photographer uses.
29. Will the photographer supply a written contract?
30. Does the written contract provide all the essential elements (see the essential elements list below)?
31. Does the photographer allow family members and guests to take photographs at the wedding?

❖ Busy Bride ❖ if the photographer doesn't pass your preliminary interview questions, then pass on that photographer.

After meeting with three or more photographers and asking them the interview questions I provided above, you should know which photographer you want to commit to. The next step is to review the photographer's written contract and check for all the essential elements.

❖ Busy Bride ❖ below is a checklist of the essential elements that should be found in your written contract with the wedding photographer:

1. The photographer's name, address, and phone numbers (the photographer who's actually photographing your wedding)
2. Your name (Busy Bride), address, and phone numbers
3. Your groom's name, address, and phone numbers
4. The addresses of the wedding and reception sites (as well as any other locations you want photographs taken), the dates, and the times that the photographer will arrive and depart the sites in order to cover all aspects of your wedding

5. The name and contact information for the emergency, or backup, photographer

6. The name of the assistant and any other staff covering your wedding

7. All services provided related to the photography package purchased

8. Schedule of fees

9. Price list for additional prints

10. Any additional costs

11. Deposit policy

12. Date of the first deposit, amount of the first deposit, and amount still owed

13. Cancellation policy

14. Any guarantees

15. Time schedule for delivery of proofs, prints, and albums

16. Your signatures (Busy Bride and Groom) and the date, and the photographer's signature and the date

After the written wedding photography contract successfully passes the essential elements test, you, your groom, and the photographer may sign and date the contract. I recommend signing two copies of the contract, one for your records and one for the photographer's records. Now relax. As long as you followed all my advice from above, you have made an intelligent decision.

❖ **Busy Bride** ❖ stop. Keep in mind that the best wedding photographer's schedule fills up fast, so book as early as possible. I recommend you start interviewing photographers at least twelve months or more before the wedding, and book your wedding photographer at least nine to twelve months before the wedding. Waste no time in searching for your wedding photographer. Remember, you deserve nothing but the best, so don't settle for the first photographer you interview.

Your wedding photographs will be all you have at the end of the big day. So make sure you give the photographer a "must photograph" list. This way you can make sure the photographer captures those essential photographs that you just can't live without.

❖ **Busy Bride** ❖ your work is done. Below is an example wedding "must photograph" checklist. You can copy it, add to it, or delete from it. The essential framework is done, so use it.

Before the wedding ceremony photographs:
- ❖ The bridal gown draped or hanging with your shoes
- ❖ The bridal bouquet
- ❖ Zipping up or buttoning the wedding dress
- ❖ Bride and attendants getting ready
- ❖ Bride's garter

- ❖ Bride's veil
- ❖ Bride looking out the window
- ❖ Bride and attendants
- ❖ Bride and mother
- ❖ Bride and flower girl
- ❖ Bride and father
- ❖ Bride and both parents
- ❖ Bride's close-up, alone, and full length
- ❖ Groom's close-up, alone, and full length
- ❖ Groom and attendants getting ready
- ❖ Pinning of the corsages and boutonnieres
- ❖ Groom and father
- ❖ Groom and mother
- ❖ Groom and both parents
- ❖ Groom and attendants
- ❖ Groom and ring bearer
- ❖ Groom leaving for the wedding ceremony
- ❖ Bride leaving for the wedding ceremony

Wedding ceremony photographs:
- ❖ Exterior and interior of the site before guests arrive
- ❖ Officiant
- ❖ Ceremony musicians
- ❖ Ceremony program
- ❖ Guest book, or signature item, and pen
- ❖ Guests signing in
- ❖ Ushers seating guests
- ❖ Parents and grandparents being seated

❖ Bride's arrival

❖ Groom waiting at the altar

❖ Wedding processional

❖ Wide shot of the back of the bride walking down the aisle

❖ Front of the bride being walked down the aisle

❖ The bride being given away

❖ Wide shot of altar during the ceremony

❖ Wide shot of the wedding party members at the altar

❖ Kneeling at the altar

❖ Lighting of the unity candles

❖ Exchanging of the rings

❖ Exchanging of the vows

❖ Other special ceremony features

❖ First kiss after married

❖ Bride and groom leading recessional

❖ Recessional

❖ Bride and groom during receiving line

❖ Guests throwing rice or other items at the bride and groom

❖ Bride's and groom's hands displaying their wedding rings over the bride's bouquet

❖ Bride and groom signing marriage license

❖ Bride and groom getting into the exit transportation

❖ Bride and groom exiting

Formal portraits:

- ❖ Bride alone (full length)
- ❖ Bride with back of the dress details
- ❖ Groom alone (full length)
- ❖ Bride and groom together
- ❖ Bride and maid or matron of honor
- ❖ Bride and other attendants
- ❖ Groom and best man
- ❖ Groom and other attendants
- ❖ Bride and groom with both sets of parents
- ❖ Bride and groom with bride's parents
- ❖ Bride and groom with groom's parents
- ❖ Bride and groom with whole wedding party
- ❖ Bride, groom, wedding party, and both parents
- ❖ Bride, groom, and bride's grandparents
- ❖ Bride, groom, and groom's grandparents
- ❖ Bride, groom, and both sets of grandparents
- ❖ Ring bearer and flower girl
- ❖ Bride and groom with ring bearer and flower girl
- ❖ Bride and groom with officiant
- ❖ Bride and groom kissing
- ❖ Bride and groom with bride's siblings
- ❖ Bride and groom with groom's siblings
- ❖ Bride and groom with bride's entire family
- ❖ Bride and groom with groom's entire family

Reception photographs:

- ❖ Exterior and interior of reception site before the guests arrive

❖ Table settings
❖ Table centerpieces
❖ Guests signing guest book or signature item
❖ Place card table
❖ Close-up of bride's and groom's place cards
❖ Head table with wedding party
❖ Specific decorations
❖ DJ or live band
❖ Wedding cake
❖ Groom's cake
❖ Bride and groom arriving
❖ Wedding party arriving
❖ Food and bar at cocktail hour
❖ Guests at tables
❖ Bride and groom's first dance
❖ Toasts
❖ Father-daughter dance
❖ Mother-son dance
❖ Guests dancing
❖ Buffet or dinner being served
❖ Groom retrieving garter
❖ Groom tossing garter
❖ Bride throwing bouquet
❖ Garter-bouquet dance
❖ Bride and groom cutting the cake
❖ Bride and groom feeding each other cake
❖ Favors
❖ Dessert table
❖ Bridal portrait display

- ❖ Gift table
- ❖ Decorating the getaway car
- ❖ Bride and groom getting into their exit transportation
- ❖ Bride and groom exiting

❖ 𝕭𝖚𝖘𝖞 𝕭𝖗𝖎𝖉𝖊 ❖ stop. Personalize your wedding "must photograph" checklist with your own ideas. This will make your wedding photographs even more fabulous.

Last word of advice, it never hurts to have your own backup photographer. Even if the person is an amateur. Find a teenager or relative willing to be paid to photograph your wedding in addition to your professional photographer. Offer your amateur fifty dollars or seventy-five dollars for taking the backup photographs. This is a great win-win situation, because the amateur is happy to get some extra money, and you are happy to receive some additional inexpensive photographs to add to your professional photographer's photographs.

Twenty-Two

Videographer

Bring sight, sound, and emotion to your wedding memories with your very own wedding video. The events of your wedding will speed by in a flash, so I strongly recommend hiring a professional wedding videographer to capture, preserve, and keep these fabulous moments alive for you forever. A wedding video also allows you and your husband to listen and to watch yourselves recite your vows on every anniversary, and it allows you to show your children and their children, the generations to come, that most memorable day in your lives. Your wedding video will be treasured as a family heirloom that captured the beginning of the union between you and your husband.

For all the reasons above, Busy Bride, you should take your time when shopping for a professional wedding videographer. I recommend interviewing at least three or more videographers before making a decision.

Before interviewing your videographers, you need to decide what type of video format you would like your wedding video to take. Video formats and combinations are endless. Below are the basic video formats:

Classic traditional, or straight shot, format is shot like a family video. Generally this format is shot with only one video camera and has no editing, no special effects, and no moving sceneries, just straight linear videotaping.

Documentary, or journalistic, format is generally shot like a documentary of an event. This format shows your wedding as it actually happens with the exact sequence of events and time. Sometimes interviews of family members and friends are added in. The video is generally edited to produce a more polished production.

Cinematic format is shot like a motion picture. Generally this format is a short highlight of your wedding day put to background music in place of your actual wedding day sounds.

It is not a question of one format being better than another, but a matter of personal style and taste. You will know the right format for your wedding video when you view samples.

❖ Busy Bride ❖ stop for two reminders. Reminder one, you should start interviewing videographers at least twelve or more months before the wedding date. Decide and book a videographer no later than nine to twelve months before the wedding. Reminder two, your videographer's budget should be no larger than five percent of the total wedding budget. So Busy Bride, get your calculator and do the math.

The next step is the videographer interview process. Knowing what to ask the videographer ahead of time will ensure a productive interview.

❖ Busy Bride ❖ stop. Your work is done. Below is a complete list of the essential questions to ask during your interviews with videographers.

1. Is the videographer available on your wedding date?
2. How long has the videographer been in business?
3. How many weddings has the videographer filmed before?
4. Does the videographer have a preferred video format, or is the choice yours?
5. Is he or she the one who will be videotaping the wedding? If no, ask to meet the videographer who will actually videotape the wedding.

6. What kind of background and education does the videographer have?

7. How many cameras does the videographer use?

8. What type of cameras does the videographer use?

9. Does the videographer have backup equipment in case of an emergency?

10. Does the videographer schedule multiple events for the same day or weekend?

11. What kind of lighting will he or she use?

12. What kind of microphones will he or she use?

13. Can you watch the videographer's most recent wedding video samples?

14. How many staff members will assist the videographer in covering a wedding?

15. What type of editing process does the videographer use?

16. Ask the videographer if he or she has worked with your chosen photographer before.

17. Will the video be placed on a DVD?

18. Has the videographer ever filmed at your ceremony reception site before? If yes, ask if you could view the video.

19. How much does the videographer charge? Hourly? Project based?

20. Can the videographer put together custom packages?

21. Can the videographer provide a written contract and guarantee?
22. Any additional costs?

Once you have completed your videographer interviews, narrow it down to your favorite one. Make sure you select someone with a proper personality for the position. Busy Bride, you need to keep in mind that the best videographers' schedules fill up fast, so reserve your videographer as early as possible.

The next step is to review the videographer's written contract and check for all the essential elements.

❖ 𝔅usy 𝔅ride ❖ below is a checklist of the essential elements that should be found in your written contract with your wedding videographer:

1. Videographer's name, address, and phone numbers (the actual videographer who's videotaping your wedding)
2. Your name (Busy Bride), address, and phone numbers
3. Your groom's name, address, and phone numbers
4. The videographer's itinerary with the dates, times, addresses of the sites he or she will be filming at, and phone numbers

5. The name and contact information for the emergency, or backup, videographer
6. The names of the videographer's assistants attending the ceremony and reception
7. All services provided related to the video package purchased
8. Schedule of fees
9. Price list for additional videos
10. Any additional costs
11. Deposit policy
12. Date of first deposit, amount of the first deposit, and amount still owed
13. Cancellation policy
14. Any guarantees
15. Time schedule for delivery of video
16. Your signatures (Busy Bride and Groom) and the date, and the videographer's signature and the date

After the written videographer's contract successfully passes the essential elements test, you, your groom, and the videographer may sign and date the contract. Don't forget to date it. I recommend signing two copies of the contract, one for your records and one for the videographer's records. Now relax. As long as you have followed all my advice from above, you have made an intelligent decision.

❖ **Busy Bride** ❖ keep in mind that your wedding video preserves the voices, the laughter, the joyful tears, the music, and not just how everyone looked. Your wedding video will bring your wedding day back to life again and again. Think of it as an investment that you and your groom will cherish for a lifetime.

Twenty-Three

Flowers

$\mathcal{B}$ usy Bride, before choosing flowers for your wedding, you need to refer back to the photographs you took at the ceremony and reception sites. Review the photographs and note where you would like entryway arbors, sprays, arrangements, centerpieces, additional foliage, and more. Incorporate your wedding color palette, theme, formality, bridal gown, and personal style into your flower choices. For example, if your colors are red, silver, and white, then yellow daisies would not be a good choice for the flowers. Red roses would be an excellent flower choice because red roses coordinate with your dominant color—red.

❖ Busy Bride ❖ stop. You can save money by choosing flowers that are in season, therefore cheaper, on the date of your wedding. The flowers below are organized by seasons:

- ❖ **Summer**—baby's breath, hydrangea, iris, calla lily, carnation, chrysanthemum, lilac, violet, daisy
- ❖ **Spring**—sweet pea, tulip, rose, lilac, cherry blossom, daffodil
- ❖ **Fall**—autumn leaves, marigold, lily, sunflower, rose, chinaberry, Queen Anne's lace
- ❖ **Winter**—camellia, 'Gerber' daisy, Queen Anne's lace, rose, pansy, holly, poinsettia, evergreen

Your flowers should create a "wow" factor for your guests. When your guests enter the ceremony and reception sites, they should think "wow" red roses or "wow" lavender lilacs. Keep in mind that bigger is always better. Remember, with proper placement your flowers will pop against the site décor. If you need help with proper placement, you can ask your floral designer for his or her advice.

Look through wedding magazines to find the flower arrangements you want at your wedding. Even if the colors are off, you should bring the flower arrangement magazine photos you've found with you when you interview different floral designers. A picture can tell a thousand words, and the florist will be extremely pleased to have a visual of what you want. Also, you should bring your wedding color palette and photos of the ceremony and reception sites to show the florist. He or she may have some ideas for flowers you didn't consider. Make sure your flower vision is clear with your chosen floral designer before signing any agreements, or contracts, and before you make your first down payment.

Before you meet with your chosen floral designer, you should review the wedding flower checklist below. The checklist will give you an idea of what type and how many wedding flowers you may need. The checklist will also help you to plan ahead and stay within your budget. Remember, your floral budget is ten percent of the total wedding budget. That ten percent covers all flowers and decorations. Below is a general list of flowers to have at your wedding. You may need more, less, or no flowers at all. The choice is yours.

Wedding Flower Checklist

(On the lines below, fill in how many of each item you will need.)

Wedding party:

_____ Bride's bouquet

_____ Bride's throwaway bouquet

_____ Bride's hair flowers

_____ Maid or matron of honor's and bridesmaids' bouquets

_____ Maid or matron of honor's and bridesmaids' hair flowers

_____ Flower girl's bouquet

_____ Flower girl's hair and basket flowers

_____ Groom's boutonniere

_____ Best man's and groomsmen's boutonnieres

_____ Ring bearer's boutonniere

_____ Ushers' boutonnieres

_____ Mother's and mother-in-law's corsages

_____ Additional special guests' corsages

_____ Father's and father-in-law's boutonnieres

_____ Additional special guests' boutonnieres

_____ Additional flowers not mentioned above

Ceremony:

_____ Altar, chuppah, or central arbor arrangements

_____ Entryway arrangements

_____ Spray arrangements

_____ Chair or pew decorations
_____ Candles and candelabras
_____ Aisle runner petals and decorations
_____ Honored chair decorations of relatives not
present at ceremony
_____ Additional flowers for ceremony not
mentioned above

Reception:

_____ Entryway arrangements
_____ Spray arrangements
_____ Guest table centerpieces
_____ Wedding party table centerpieces
_____ Bride's and groom's chair decorations
_____ Bar decorations
_____ Hors d'oeuvre table decorations
_____ Buffet table decorations
_____ Cake and cake table decorations
_____ Dessert table decorations
_____ Gift table decorations
_____ Photo memory table decorations
_____ Restroom decorations
_____ Additional flowers needed for the wedding
cake
_____ Additional flowers for reception not
mentioned above

The bridal bouquet is known as the one
tradition that is present at almost all weddings, even

the most original and unconventional weddings. The bridal bouquet tradition originally started as a way for brides to use strong smelling flowers and herbs to ward off evil sprits on their wedding day. Today, brides no longer choose bridal bouquet flowers because of the flowers' strong smells, but because the flowers coordinate with the bride's wedding theme, color palette, formality, bridal gown, and personal style.

Busy Bride, the bridal bouquet will make the boldest statement, so it should be the biggest bouquet with the most fabulous flowers you can afford. Make sure your floral designer wraps all your bouquets in the same coordinating colored ribbon, foil, or fabric for a polished presentation. Don't forget to order a cheap throwaway bouquet for the bridal toss. The throwaway bouquet should be a smaller version of your real bridal bouquet.

There are tons and tons of different bridal bouquet styles, but the three most popular and basic styles are the round, cascade, and hand-tied bouquets.

The round bouquet, also known as the tussie-mussie, nosegay, or posy bouquet, is made up of mostly flowers that are shaped into a smooth ball.

The outer perimeter of the bouquet is generally edged in greenery. By far, this is the most popular bouquet style. It's also my favorite style. It can be used in both formal and informal weddings.

The cascade bouquet is shaped like a waterfall with more flowers at the top and less and less as the flowers flow downward. I recommend this bouquet style for a more formal wedding.

The hand-tied bouquet has no distinct shape. It is composed by tying a ribbon around a simple bunch of flowers and leaving the stems exposed. I recommend this bouquet style for a more casual wedding.

❖ *Busy Bride* ❖ when selecting your bridal bouquet style please keep these four items in mind:

1. Your wedding formality and theme
2. Your bridal gown style
3. Your personal style
4. The statement you want to make

Your bridal bouquet is the most important accessory you will have on your wedding day. Make sure it is a fabulous accent piece that accentuates your beautiful bridal gown.

Fabulous flowers are the key to transforming an ordinary banquet room into a wonderful wedding reception venue. As your guests find their tables and sit down, the first things they will notice are your centerpieces. The centerpieces are usually placed on all guest tables, buffet tables, hors d'oeuvre tables, the gift table, and any additional areas a centerpiece would be aesthetically pleasing. Your centerpieces should add color, texture, and fragrance to your wedding reception leaving your guests with a lasting impression of how beautiful your reception looked.

I recommend interviewing at least two to three floral designers before you make your decision. Remember, a great floral designer is essential when choosing fabulous flowers. Make sure the floral designer actually specializes in weddings and doesn't just run the local flower shop. Don't be afraid to ask the floral designer some questions.

❖ Busy Bride ❖ below is a list of interview questions to ask during your interviews with floral designers:

1. How many years of floral design experience does the floral designer have?
2. Does the floral designer have any photos of other weddings he or she has done?

3.   Does the floral designer have any photos of bouquet and arrangement styles?

4.   What type of formal training or education does the floral designer have in floral design?

5.   How many weddings a year does the floral designer service?

6.   Will he or she be the floral designer doing your floral arrangements and décor?

7.   Does the floral designer have a backup or replacement floral designer in case of an emergency?

8.   Can the floral designer provide any references?

9.   Has he or she serviced any other weddings at your ceremony or reception sites?

10. Does the floral designer have a website?

11. What are the floral designer's prices, and what types of packages or discounts does he or she offer?

12. What does the floral designer's contract contain? Ask to see a copy. Does the contract provide for all the essential elements (see the essential elements list below)?

13. What other additional fees does the floral designer charge?

After meeting with at least two to three floral designers and asking them the interview questions I provided above, you should know which floral designer you want to commit to. The next step is to review the contract and check for all the essential elements.

❖ **Busy Bride** ❖ below is a checklist of essential elements that should be found in your written contract with the wedding floral designer. Keep in mind that if the floral designer does not put something in writing, it generally means he or she won't do it.

1. The floral designer's name, address, and phone numbers (the actual floral designer servicing your wedding)
2. Your name (Busy Bride), address, and phone numbers
3. Your groom's name, address, and phone numbers
4. The date of the wedding
5. The date, times, and locations for floral arrangements and décor to be delivered to the wedding party, ceremony site, and reception site
6. The name and contact information for the emergency, or backup, floral designer
7. All services provided related to flowers, decorations, and any additional services
8. Schedule of fees
9. Additional costs

10. Deposit policy
11. Date of first deposit, amount of first deposit, and amount still owed
12. Cancellation policy
13. Any guarantees
14. Your signatures (Busy Bride and Groom) and the date, and the floral designer's signature and the date

After the written floral contract successfully passes the essential elements test, you, your groom, and the floral designer may sign and date the contract. I recommend signing two copies of the contract, one for your records and one for the floral designer's records. Now relax. As long as you have followed my advice from above, you have made an intelligent decision.

❖ **Busy Bride** ❖ stop. When picking out your flowers, you should think fabulous, elegant, classy, and the more flowers the more fabulous. Keep in mind that your wedding is a day you will cherish and remember forever, so go all out.

Twenty-Four

Wedding Cake

The wedding cake is the second biggest focal point of the guests' attentions at the reception. The bride is always the first. Some brides choose cakes so large it's like the cake is looking down on the guests. Busy Bride, you should never think just ordinary when planning your wedding cake. Always think extraordinary!

The first step in the wedding cake process is to gather magazine photos of cakes. These photos don't have to show whole cakes with the perfect colors, styles, or designs like you want for your wedding cake. The photos can just show elements you like.

Once you've gathered photos with the cake elements you like, you need to narrow down your selections with your groom. For example, after narrowing down your selections, you might have one photo showing an example of the cake shape you would like and another photo showing an example of the color or design you want on your cake. Bring these cake photos, your theme, color palette, flower choices, cake budget, and the approximate number of guests you expect to the cake designer appointment. This will make your appointment as stress free as possible and the cake designer will be extremely pleased.

❖ Busy Bride ❖ stop. You can save yourself time and money by asking the right questions at your cake designer appointment. These questions and tips will help eliminate any hidden charges and help you stay informed and knowledgeable.

1. How long has the cake designer been in business?
2. Ask to taste the cake flavors and fillings.
3. Ask to view other wedding cakes the cake designer has done.
4. What type of package prices does the cake designer offer?
5. Ask about extra costs.
6. Does the cake designer charge for delivery or setup?
7. Does the cake designer have a back-up or replacement designer in case of an emergency?
8. Ask about the cake designer's deposit policy.
9. Always ask for a written contract.

After meeting with your cake designer and asking him or her the interview questions I provided above, you should know if you want to commit. The next step is to review the contract and check for all the essential elements.

❖ 𝔅usy 𝔅ride ❖ below is a checklist of essential elements that should be found in your written contract with the cake designer. Keep in mind that if the cake designer does not put something in writing, it generally means he or she won't do it.

1. The cake designer's name, address, and phone numbers (the actual cake designer servicing your wedding)
2. Your name (Busy Bride), address, and phone numbers
3. Your groom's name, address, and phone numbers
4. The date of the wedding
5. The date, time, and location for the cake to be delivered to the reception site
6. The name and contact information for the emergency, or backup, cake designer
7. All services provided related to wedding cake and any additional services
8. Schedule of fees
9. Additional costs
10. Deposit policy
11. Date of first deposit, amount of first deposit, and amount still owed

12. Cancellation policy
13. Any guarantees
14. Your signatures (Busy Bride and Groom) and the date, and the cake designer's signature and the date

After you have reviewed the written contract and it contains all the essential elements above, you and the cake designer may sign and date the contract.

The average wedding cake slice ranges from two dollars to four dollars and fifty cents. Wedding cupcakes, sometimes referred to as *mini cakes*, are a less expensive option. They usually cost anywhere from one dollar and fifty cents to two dollars each. Choose the option that best fits your formality, theme, budget, and personal style.

❖ Busy Bride ❖ stop. Here's a fabulous wedding cake secret your guests will never know . . . If you're the type of busy bride who's always dreamed of having a huge towering cake, but you don't need the extra layers of cake or your budget won't allow it, then ask your cake designer to replace a layer or two with frosted Styrofoam. Your guests will never know, and you won't destroy your budget.

Twenty-Five

Transportation

The most common wedding transportation is traditionally the limousine. Today, however, more and more couples are choosing more inventive, dramatic, and memorable transportation methods. Busy Bride, you will need transportation to the ceremony, photographic and reception sites, and then you will need transportation to the wedding night hotel or escape to your honeymoon. Other factors to keep in mind when choosing your wedding transportation are the size of your wedding party, your wedding theme, your color palette, your wedding attire, and any additional family members (like your parents) who will also need wedding transportation.

❖ **Busy Bride** ❖ stop. Remember, your wedding transportation should cost no more than three percent of your total wedding budget. So shop around for the best price before you sign any contracts.

Depending on your reception and ceremony locations, you may also need to provide mass transportation for your wedding guests. In this case, you may want to rent larger vehicles, such as RVs, trolley cars, or even double-decker buses to transport your wedding guests.

❖ **Busy Bride** ❖ stop. Your work is done. Below is a list of my favorite wedding transportation options you may want to consider:

- ❖ Hot air balloon
- ❖ Hummer
- ❖ Elephant
- ❖ Four-wheeler
- ❖ Limo bus
- ❖ Fire truck
- ❖ Tractor-trailer
- ❖ Van
- ❖ Party bus
- ❖ Trolley car
- ❖ Horse and buggy
- ❖ Snowmobile
- ❖ Motorcycle
- ❖ Retro car
- ❖ Vintage car
- ❖ Regular limo
- ❖ Town car
- ❖ Sleigh
- ❖ Plane
- ❖ Luxury car

- Glider
- Parade float
- Unicycle
- School bus
- Helicopter
- Golf cart
- Bicycle for two
- Scooter

❖ **Busy Bride** ❖ stop. You can save money with my recommended wedding transportation tips:

- Only rent fabulous wedding transportation for the grand entrance and getaway.
- Eliminate the extras such as TVs, sunroof, bar, or any other add-on amenities.
- Choose the standard limo, or vehicle, instead of the stretch.
- Choose a black or silver vehicle as these are generally less expensive color choices.
- Book your wedding transportation at least six months or more before the wedding date. You can generally receive a discount for booking ahead.
- Shop in your area for the best price and wedding transportation options.
- Require the transportation company to provide a written contract outlining its services.

Busy Bride, the last thing you need to do is create a transportation wedding day schedule. The schedule should include a list of everyone being transported, pickup times, drop off times, detailed directions to all addresses, and any emergency contact information. Make copies of the transportation schedule and distribute them to the transportation company, wedding party, and family members.

Utilize your wedding transportation to indulge in something you normally wouldn't think of riding in or on. Think outside the box. Choose wedding transportation that will "wow" your guests and have them talking for years to come.

Twenty-Six

Rental Items

Why buy it when you can rent it? Rental service companies provide wedding ceremony and reception items at a fraction of the item's cost. From tents to candelabras these companies supply the necessary equipment to create that fabulous celebration atmosphere you have been imagining since he proposed to you.

When planning an unconventional wedding ceremony and reception site, like ones with a beach or mountainside theme, a rental service company will be an essential tool in meeting all your wedding needs whether complex or simple.

❖ **Busy Bride** ❖ stop. Remember, the budget for the additional rental items falls under the reception budget. The total reception budget is fifty percent of the total wedding budget. So get a calculator and do the math to see what you have to spend.

Busy Bride, the first step in choosing a rental service company is to ask around for referrals. Ask your other vendors if they recommend using any particular company. Also, check the phone book for rental service company ads. Generally, the larger the ad, the better the company. The second step is to meet with a few rental service companies and ask to see their list of available items, costs, rental agreement, payment schedule, additional costs, delivery costs, setup costs, teardown costs, and transportation costs. Make sure the company can rent you all the items you will need for the wedding ceremony and reception sites.

The variety of possible rental items can be endless, so don't get carried away. Rent only what you will need and always keep your budget in mind. In the end, if you have extra money left in your budget, you can always call your rental service company and add-in that extra over-the-top item like a photo booth or money machine.

❖ 𝔅usy 𝔅ride ❖ below is a basic list of ceremony and reception rental items. You can add or delete items as needed.

Basic wedding ceremony rental items:
- ❖ Aisle runner
- ❖ Kneeling benches or cushions
- ❖ Arch structure
- ❖ Chuppah

- ❖ Audio equipment
- ❖ Candelabras
- ❖ Silk plants
- ❖ Candles
- ❖ Candle lighters
- ❖ Guest chairs
- ❖ Heaters
- ❖ Air conditioning units
- ❖ Guest book stand
- ❖ Tent or canopy
- ❖ Lighting package

Basic wedding reception rental items:
- ❖ Tent or canopy
- ❖ Dance floor
- ❖ Tables
- ❖ Chairs
- ❖ Chair covers
- ❖ Linens
- ❖ Tableware
- ❖ Heaters
- ❖ Air conditioning units
- ❖ Lanterns
- ❖ Lighting package
- ❖ Trash cans
- ❖ Gift table
- ❖ Audio equipment
- ❖ Silk plants
- ❖ Platforms and staging
- ❖ Portable bar

Twenty-Seven

Stationery

Busy Bride, the first glimpse your guests will receive of your fabulous upcoming wedding will be a save-the-date. If you choose not to send a save-the-date, then your wedding invitation will serve as your guests' first glimpse. Either way, both pieces, and your entire wedding stationery, should coordinate with your wedding theme, formality, and color palette. Your wedding stationery will set the tone for your wedding.

Your guests will rely on your wedding stationery to tell them the proper dress to wear and what they can expect at your wedding. For example, your guests will have no idea you're having a Las Vegas themed wedding if they receive a traditional save-the-date and wedding invitation. So make sure your wedding stationery reflects the type of affair your guests will be attending, that way everyone is prepared, comfortable, and ready to enjoy themselves.

When shopping for wedding stationery, don't be afraid to ask for samples. Most stationery companies will be happy to provide three or four samples of your favorite stationery selections. I recommend setting the samples up side-by-side and comparing their qualities. Feel free to ask friends or family members for their opinions. Just keep in mind that it's your wedding, and you should make the final decision based on what you want.

Wedding stationery isn't just the save-the-dates and wedding invitations. There are other elements too, like table cards, menu cards, thank-you cards, napkins, ceremony programs, and so much more. I recommend ordering your wedding stationery twelve months or more before a destination wedding and nine to twelve months before a local wedding. Below is a list of possible wedding stationery items you may want for your wedding. I recommend reviewing this list before you place any orders.

Wedding stationery items:
❖ Save-the-dates
❖ Wedding invitations
❖ Inner wedding invitation envelopes
❖ Response cards
❖ Response card envelopes
❖ Invitation tissue paper(Used to protect the invitation.)
❖ Reception invitation cards
❖ Outer wedding invitation envelopes
❖ Directions or map cards or both

- ❖ Thank-you cards
- ❖ Ceremony programs
- ❖ Wedding rehearsal and rehearsal dinner invitations
- ❖ Wedding rehearsal and rehearsal dinner invitation envelopes
- ❖ Rehearsal dinner menu cards
- ❖ Reception place cards
- ❖ Reception table cards
- ❖ Reception menu cards
- ❖ Signature wedding cocktail menu cards
- ❖ Personalized cocktail napkins
- ❖ Personalized stir sticks
- ❖ Personalized favor bags or boxes
- ❖ Personalized cake take-home boxes
- ❖ Personalized tumblers
- ❖ Personalized coasters
- ❖ Personalized matchbooks
- ❖ Personalized ribbons
- ❖ Personalized stickers
- ❖ Any additional personalized wedding stationery items not mentioned above

❖ **Busy Bride** ❖ stop. Take a deep breath. Don't feel overwhelmed by all the wedding stationery choices or the proper wedding etiquette that should be followed. Choosing and ordering your wedding stationery is not something I recommend doing in fifteen minutes. Plan to spend a few hours, days, or even weeks choosing your stationery, wording the stationery pieces properly, choosing your printing method, choosing your paper, choosing your ink colors, and ordering all your stationery pieces so they all coordinate and complete your fabulous wedding stationery.

When ordering your wedding stationery, I recommend having the following items below nearby:

1. The name, address, date, and time of your ceremony rehearsal
2. The name, address, date, and time of your rehearsal dinner
3. Rehearsal dinner menu
4. The name, address, date, and time of your wedding ceremony
5. The name, address, date, and time of your wedding reception
6. Reception dinner menu
7. Artwork for maps or direction verbiage
8. Ceremony program information
9. Signature wedding cocktail menu
10. The amount of each stationery piece that needs to be ordered

Busy Bride, you need to keep in mind that when counting your save-the-dates or wedding invitations, you don't count each guest as one. Count a couple or a family in one household as one wedding stationery piece. I recommend ordering extra stationery in case you make a mistake when writing the addresses on the envelopes or extra guests need to be invited.

❖ **Busy Bride** ❖ when you're addressing the invitation envelopes write "and family" if the children are also invited. See my examples below:

Children not invited
Mr. and Mrs. Ken Ferria

Children invited
Mr. and Mrs. Ken Ferria and Family

❖ **Busy Bride** ❖ when addressing the invitation envelopes to your single friends and family members always add "and guest," so they understand they can bring a guest if they choose to. See my examples below:

Mr. Christopher Dello and Guest

or

Miss Adrianna Rose and Guest

Inside your invitation you should place your response card and stamped response card envelope.

This lets your guests know you expect a confirmation of their presence. Don't expect to receive all your response cards back, generally about twenty-five percent of your guests won't return the response card. I recommend calling the guests you have not received a response card from to confirm if they are coming or not.

Proper etiquette for the wedding invitation envelopes is to handwrite or calligraphy all your guests' addresses. I recommend setting aside enough time to address a few invitations at a time to ensure the quality of the writing. Another option is to find someone who provides wedding calligraphy services and hire the individual.

Here are my last words of wedding stationery wisdom . . . Keep in mind that your wedding stationery should mirror the mood you want to create on your fabulous wedding day. The more personalized your wedding stationery design, the more memorable an impression your stationery will have on your guests.

Twenty-Eight

Ceremony Program

The wedding ceremony program is one of those extra details that adds a personal touch to your dream day event, so you can remember it forever. Your program will help your guests understand what is happening and feel involved in the ceremony. It also provides a souvenir or keepsake for all your guests to remember one of the most important events of your life. As each guest enters the ceremony site, he or she should receive a wedding ceremony program, generally from an usher.

❖ Busy Bride ❖ stop. Remember to add your own personal and creative touch to every aspect of your special day. This will "wow" your guests. .

The ceremony program wording should clearly explain the sequence of events during the ceremony, almost like a meeting agenda. It should contain four parts. The first part should contain a brief introduction, with your full names as bride and groom, the date, the time, the location, and any additional special remarks.

The second part should contain the prelude and solo music, lighting of the candles, seating procession, invocation, wedding message, exchange of vows, exchange of rings, announcement of marriage, presentation of the bride and groom, and recessional music. You might also want to include the titles of the music selected, lyrics, or words of prayer. It is not essential to have all, or any, of the above included in your wedding ceremony or program. Some couples choose less. Some couples choose more. In the end, the choice is totally up to the couple.

The third part of the wedding ceremony program is the explanation of the wedding party. Generally, the wedding party is written in this order: the bride's parents, followed by the groom's parents, then the bride's grandparents, the groom's grandparents, the maid or matron of honor, the best man, the bridesmaids, the groomsmen, the flower girl, the ring bearer, the pianist, the soloist, and anyone else in the wedding party.

The forth part should include words of thanks to your guests and wedding party, dedications to your parents and deceased family members, and any other additional words. Some couples choose to include reception instructions.

❖ 𝕭𝖚𝖘𝖞 𝕭𝖗𝖎𝖉𝖊 ❖ your work is done. Below is an example wedding ceremony program. Add your own personal and creative touch for extra dazzling pizzazz.

𝕻𝖆𝖗𝖙 I

> (Busy Bride, do not include "Part" titles in your program. They're to show you the parts I mentioned above.)

The marriage service of

Amy Lynn Applebottom

and

Dominic Joseph Fierra

Friday, May 18, 2010

4:30 PM

The Michael Angelo House and Gardens

Weddingville, New Jersey

℘art II

Prelude
Adagio from Sonata in E-flat
by Mozart

Seating of honored guests
"Air" from *Water Music*
by Handel

Processional
"Trumpet Voluntary
(The Prince of Denmark's March)"
by Jeremiah Clarke

Bride's entrance
"Wedding March"
from *Lohengrin*by Wagner

Wedding message
Reverend Christopher David Blesso

Exchange of rings

Lighting of unity candle

Pronouncement and introduction of husband and wife

Recessional
> "Wedding March" from
> *A Midsummer Night's Dream*
> by Mendelssohn

Part III

The wedding party

The bride's parents
> Scott and Sandy Applebottom

The groom's parents
> Tom and Dina Fierra

The bride's grandparents
> Steve and Shirley Applebottom

The groom's grandparents
> Gregory and Tracey Fierra

Maid of honor
> Danella Cece

Best man
> Fred Stone

Bridesmaids
> Jenny Smith
> Ashley Applebottom (sister of bride)

Groomsmen
> Jason Smith
> Ken Fierra (brother of groom)

Flower girl
> Bella Applebottom (niece of bride)

Ring bearer
> Simon Smith

Pianist
> Anna Carey

Part IV

Thank you for all your love, support, and most of all, being here with us to share in this fabulous day.

Amy Lynn and Dominic

❖ **Busy Bride** ❖ remember to design your wedding ceremony program at least two months or more before the wedding. Then print your ceremony programs about a month before your fabulous wedding day.

Twenty-Nine

Reception Seating Chart

C reating a formal reception seating chart can be a difficult task, but it is an essential tool in ensuring a successful reception for you and your guests. Busy Bride, your first step is to visualize your reception site layout. If you need to, you can refer back to the photographs you took during your reception site appointment.

The second step is to plan out your areas. You need one area for the entertainer, one for the cake table, one for the gift table, one for the hors d'oeuvre table, one for the buffet table, one for the bridal party table, several areas for your guests' tables, and so on. On a sheet of paper, Busy Bride, sketch your reception room and add in all the areas mentioned above. If you're not a great artist, try creating a sketch of your reception room on the computer using programs like Microsoft Publisher, Paint, or Microsoft Word.

The next step is to count the total number of RSVPs or guests attending. This will give you a better idea of how many guest tables you will need.

I recommend always adding an extra table for unexpected or last minute guests. Number or name each table on your room sketch, and then organize your guests by table numbers or names.

When your room sketch is finalized, you can then create your final reception seating chart. I recommend enlarging your chart to poster size and framing it to place at the entrance of your reception for a more fabulous presentation. If you choose to also use place cards or name cards, then have the guest's name and table number or name printed on them. Alphabetize the cards and place them on a table next to your reception seating chart.

❖ Busy Bride ❖ when planning your seating chart, never put feuding relatives or friends at the same table. Seat your guests so they have a fabulous time. Section your guests into groups. For example, place all your work colleagues together, your immediate family together, your extended family together, your church friends together, your college friends together, and so on. I recommend making your table numbers or categories large enough for even your elderly relatives to see. Believe me, you don't want your almost deaf, almost blind great Aunt Mildred causing a scene in the middle of your reception because she can't find her table.

Make seating as simple as possible for your guests. Total assigned seating is a rule of the past, so let your guests sit in the seats of their choice at their assigned table.

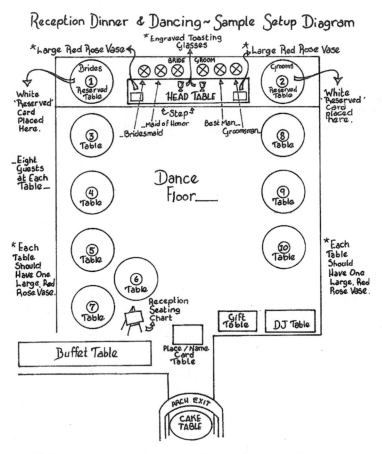

Reception Dinner & Dancing ~ Sample Setup Diagram

Using a reception seating chart will give your guests peace of mind because someone has planned a seat for them; therefore they don't have to panic and scramble looking for an available seat. Your guests' enjoyment and the success of your reception are heavily weighted on your reception seating chart, so don't take it lightly. Taking extra time planning the perfect seating for your guests will ensure an exceptionally fabulous reception for all.

Thirty

Hair, Makeup, And Nails

I sn't she lovely? is what you want whispered as you walk down the aisle. Busy Bride, the essential elements to making you look fabulous on your wedding day are hair, makeup, and nails.

Busy Bride—Hair

Busy Bride, here are the essential rules for gorgeous, thick, healthy hair. Start following the list below a year or more before your wedding:

1. Eat healthy foods
2. Exercise
3. Drink eight to ten glasses of water a day
4. Take one multivitamin a day
5. Take one biotin supplement a day (ask your doctor for recommended dosage)

Planning a wedding can be very stressful on a bride, and stress causes hair loss and breakage. So follow my essential rules and your hair will look fabulous. Remember, a healthy bride is a happy bride, so take care of yourself first and your wedding planning second.

The first step in creating your bridal hairstyle is to purchase some hair and bridal magazines. Start searching for at least two fabulous wedding hairstyles that you want your hair to look like. Always keep in mind your wedding theme, formality, bridal gown design, and neckline. All these elements should coordinate with your bridal hairstyle.

There are three basic bridal hairstyles: a full updo, a half up, and all your hair down. At least two months or more before the wedding, you should schedule a trial run hair appointment. Bring your veil, headpiece, magazine photos, bridal gown photo, and camera to the appointment. Consult with your stylist and make sure she or he understands what you expect. After the stylist has styled your hair, have her or him or a friend take some photos of your hair from the front, back, left side, and right side. At home, review and print your photos. Make sure your hairstyle is as fabulous as you planned. If not, find another stylist and redo your trial run appointment. Don't settle for an "okay" hairstyle, make sure it's exactly what you want. Only the best will do, because you are the bride and it is your wedding day. Once you have decided on a stylist, schedule your appointment for your wedding day. Book as far in advance as possible to secure your stylist and the time slot needed.

On the day of your wedding, remember to wear a shirt that buttons, zips, or a top you don't mind cutting to protect your bridal hairstyle. Pulling anything over your head after your hair is done might ruin your fabulous hairdo. Don't take any chances, plan ahead or bring your scissors. If your stylist can travel to your home or the site where you're getting ready, even better, she can do your hair while you're in your bathrobe.

Make sure your stylist

1. uses extra-hold hair spray on your hair;
2. gives you extra matching bobby pins, if your stylist used them on your bridal hairstyle;
3. knows where to meet you, if it is somewhere other than the salon;
4. schedules the proper amount of time to complete your fabulous bridal hairstyle;
5. has a replacement stylist in case of an emergency situation.

❖ Busy Bride ❖ stop for some bridal hairstyle examples:

1. If your wedding has a beach theme, I recommend a more beach-like casual hairstyle, like your hair all down or half down with loose wavy curls.

2. If your bridal gown neckline is halter, I recommend wearing your hair in an updo and showing off your beautiful neck and back.
3. If your bridal gown neckline is strapless, I recommend styling your hair all down or half down for a less revealing look.
4. If your theme is Cinderella or fairy tale with a ball gown bridal dress, I recommend a romantic soft updo to coordinate with your theme and bridal gown style.

Busy Bride—Makeup

You have chosen the dress, the shoes, the veil, the tiara, the flowers, the caterer, the photographer, and more . . . Don't wait till the last minute to choose your makeup. One of the most important aspects of the day is making sure your face looks fabulously flawless. If you're stressing and feeling pressured about your makeup, then a professional makeup artist is the right choice for you. I recommend at least one month or more before your wedding that you meet with your professional makeup artist for a trial run. Bring magazine photos of makeup you like to help make your vision clear to your artist. If you choose to use a professional makeup artist, you can hire one from a beauty salon, a department store, or one from the film and TV industry.

❖ **Busy Bride** ❖ stop and learn about the new Hollywood makeup trend. It's called airbrush makeup, and it doesn't cake or streak like traditional makeup. It lasts ten to sixteen hours and generally doesn't rub off or disappear into your skin pores. For a fabulously flawless face for your entire wedding day, this is the perfect bridal makeup.

If your budget doesn't allow for a professional makeup artist, or your control-freak personality won't allow you to surrender your face to a professional, then doing your makeup yourself is the right choice for you. If you're doing your own makeup, I recommend purchasing all your wedding makeup one month or more before the wedding. And then you need to practice, practice, practice applying your makeup like you would for the day of your wedding. Practice wearing your wedding makeup to the office or out on a Saturday night for cocktails so you can get used to wearing it. Practice touching up your makeup after you've worn it for a few hours. Remember, practice makes perfect and that is exactly how you want your fabulous face to look—absolutely perfect.

Busy Bride—Nails

Busy Bride, from your fingers to your toes, a manicure and a pedicure are both a must. A manicured hand will accentuate that sparkling engagement ring. Pampered feet from a pedicure will accentuate your bejeweled, sexy, strapped shoes, or just make you feel like the belle of the ball.

Basic nail types:
1. Natural nails
2. Acrylic nails
3. Gel nails

Basic nail shades:
1. Natural manicure (no polish)
2. French manicure
3. Colored polish

For a coordinating look, I recommend picking the same nail type and shade for both your fingers and your toes. Keep your wedding theme, formality, and bridal gown in mind when making your nail selections because everything needs to coordinate to make your wedding fabulous.

❖ Busy Bride ❖ schedule your manicure and pedicure appointment for the day before your wedding. I recommend in the morning or afternoon before your rehearsal dinner.

Thirty-One

The Honeymoon

Your honeymoon is a vacation well deserved after all the planning, organizing, and stress from your wedding. It's all about you and your groom and a vacation that meets each and every one of your wishes. Honeymoon planning should not be put off till the last minute. To make sure you get your fabulous dream destination, you should begin planning for the honeymoon just after you become engaged.

Get together with your groom and determine your desired honeymoon locations. I recommend writing down your top ten destinations. Also, write down what you want to visit and see on your honeymoon. After you and your groom have decided on your list of destinations and activities, you should visit a few travel agents. A travel agent will help you find the best honeymoon deals. Before you purchase with a travel agent, you should check for cheaper bargains online for the same trip. If the trip is unavailable online or higher priced, then use your travel agent.

❖ 𝕭𝖚𝖘𝖞 𝕭𝖗𝖎𝖉𝖊 ❖ stop. Read the tips below for saving money on your honeymoon:

1. Plan ahead. The earlier you book your honeymoon, the more you will save.
2. Set your honeymoon budget before you start shopping for your honeymoon.
3. Take a cruise. Cruises are a very cost efficient vacation, and most cruises are all-inclusive. They are even cheaper if you have a homeport close by and don't have to fly to meet the ship.
4. Don't travel far from home. The farther you travel, the more expensive the cost.
5. Don't travel too long. A five-day honeymoon is cheaper than a two-week honeymoon.
6. Travel off-season and receive the discounts.
7. Enter every free honeymoon trip contest you can find. A free trip anywhere is a fabulous trip.

❖ 𝕭𝖚𝖘𝖞 𝕭𝖗𝖎𝖉𝖊 ❖ stop. Below is a list of my favorite honeymoon vacation destinations. Sit with your groom and review this list.

- ❖ Mexico (especially Cancun)
- ❖ Italy

- ❖ Hawaii
- ❖ France
- ❖ Greece
- ❖ Jamaica
- ❖ Bermuda
- ❖ Las Vegas
- ❖ Bahamas
- ❖ New York City
- ❖ Florida
- ❖ Niagara Falls
- ❖ Aruba
- ❖ Atlantic City
- ❖ Canada

Wherever you choose to travel to, keep in mind that your honeymoon is an extended celebration of your union in marriage. So celebrate and have the time of your life, Busy Bride. Don't forget to enjoy each other and the beginning of your life together as husband and wife.

Thirty-Two

Busy Bride's Packing Lists

What to pack? Unsure about all the items you will need?

❖ **Busy Bride** ❖ stop. Your work is done. Below is a packing list for your wedding day, wedding night, and honeymoon.

Wedding Day Packing List
- ❖ Bride's wedding day survival box (see "36. Wedding Survival Boxes" for details)
- ❖ Wedding dress
- ❖ Slip
- ❖ Shoes
- ❖ Stockings
- ❖ Any additional undergarments (like bra or underwear)
- ❖ Garter
- ❖ Any additional makeup
- ❖ Jewelry
- ❖ Veil
- ❖ Hairstyle magazine photo
- ❖ Tiara
- ❖ Any additional hair items

- ❖ Marriage license
- ❖ Rings
- ❖ Purse with driver's license and about twenty dollars cash
- ❖ Wedding organizer notebook
- ❖ Cash and checks to pay vendors

Wedding Night Packing List

- ❖ Sexy lingerie
- ❖ Intimate aides
- ❖ Sexy music
- ❖ Candles and matches
- ❖ Rose petals
- ❖ Beer, wine, or champagne
- ❖ Lubricant
- ❖ Birth control method
- ❖ Toothbrush and toothpaste
- ❖ Dental floss
- ❖ Mouthwash
- ❖ Hair comb, hairbrush
- ❖ Q-Tips
- ❖ Makeup
- ❖ Makeup remover
- ❖ Facial wash
- ❖ Facial lotion
- ❖ Hair spray, hair gel
- ❖ Bras
- ❖ Underwear
- ❖ Socks
- ❖ Shampoo

❖ Conditioner
❖ Razors
❖ Deodorant
❖ Tweezers
❖ Nail clippers
❖ Small scissors
❖ Hair dryer
❖ Cell phone
❖ Cell phone charger
❖ Change of clothes
❖ Body lotion
❖ Swimsuit
❖ Tampons or pads
❖ Sunscreen
❖ Shoes (sneakers, heels, etc.)
❖ Workout clothes
❖ Workout bra

Honeymoon Packing List
❖ Hair spray, hair gel
❖ Toothbrush and toothpaste
❖ Dental floss
❖ Hair comb, hairbrush
❖ Q-Tips
❖ Small scissors
❖ Nail clippers
❖ Tweezers
❖ Blow dryer
❖ Makeup remover
❖ Facial lotion

❖ Facial wash
❖ Deodorant
❖ Hair bands
❖ Bobby pins
❖ Shampoo
❖ Conditioner
❖ Razors
❖ Body lotion
❖ Driver's license or government issued ID
❖ Cash, credit cards, traveler's checks
❖ Doctors' numbers
❖ Medications
❖ Vitamins
❖ Mini umbrella
❖ Sunscreen
❖ Disposable camera
❖ Extra tote bag
❖ Nighttime purse
❖ Nighttime wallet
❖ Daytime purse
❖ Nightgown
❖ Bras
❖ Underwear
❖ Workout clothes
❖ Workout bra
❖ Socks
❖ Shoes (sneakers, flip-flops, heels, etc.)
❖ Swimsuit
❖ Sunglasses
❖ Shorts

- ❖ Pants
- ❖ Tops
- ❖ Dresses
- ❖ Nighttime clothes
- ❖ Cell phone
- ❖ Cell phone charger
- ❖ Hard candy, gum, mints
- ❖ Snacks
- ❖ Bottled water
- ❖ Books, magazines
- ❖ Sunless tanning lotion
- ❖ Tampons or pads
- ❖ Travel itinerary
- ❖ Tickets
- ❖ Passport, for foreign travel or cruises
- ❖ Eye glasses or contacts
- ❖ Jewelry
- ❖ Intimate aides
- ❖ Any additional intimate items
- ❖ Birth control method

Thirty-Three

Signature Wedding Cocktails

E very fabulous wedding must have a signature wedding cocktail. Make sure you name your signature wedding cocktail something flirty, fun, and fabulous. Also, don't forget to incorporate your wedding theme and color palette into your signature wedding cocktail color and flavor.

❖ **Busy Bride** ❖ stop and look no further. Below is a list of flirty, fun, and fabulously named cocktails that I've created that you might want to consider using as your signature wedding cocktail.

Lady in Red—drink color: red
   4 oz. champagne
   splash of grenadine
   1 strawberry for garnish
   ice cubes
   Mixing instructions: Mix champagne and grenadine together. Pour over ice and add a strawberry to the rim of the glass for garnish.

A Wedding Willy—drink color: light orange or yellow

2 oz. coconut rum

1 oz. peach schnapps

1 oz. triple sec

2 oz. orange juice

2 oz. pineapple juice

1 orange slice for garnish

ice cubes

Mixing instructions: Mix coconut rum, peach schnapps, and triple sec. Add orange and pineapple juice to taste. Then shake with shaker and pour over ice cubes. Garnish with an orange slice on the rim of the glass.

Lusting for Love—drink color: red

4 oz. red table wine

splash of lemon-lime soda

Mixing instructions: Mix chilled red wine with splash of lemon-lime soda to taste.

Always on the Money—drink color: green (Las Vegas or casino theme)

2 oz. green melon liqueur

1 oz. vodka

4 oz. lemon-lime soda

1 cherry for garnish

ice cubes

Mixing instructions: Mix green melon liqueur, vodka, and lemon-lime soda over ice cubes. Stir and garnish with a cherry.

White Wedding Dress—drink color: white
2 oz. clear chocolate liqueur
1 oz. vodka
6 oz. milk
ice cubes

Mixing instructions: Pour clear chocolate liqueur, vodka, and milk over ice cubes in a shaker and shake. Then pour over ice cubes in a glass.

Hit by Cupid's Arrow—drink color: red (Valentine's Day theme)
1 oz. tequila
1 oz. cranberry liqueur
5 oz. cranberry juice
1 lime wedge for garnish
ice cubes

Mixing instructions: Mix tequila, cranberry liqueur, and cranberry juice over ice cubes. Stir and garnish with a lime wedge on the rim of the glass.

Something Blue—drink color: blue
2½ oz. vodka

1 oz. sweet and sour mix

1 oz. blue curaçao

3 oz. pineapple juice

1 slice of pineapple for garnish

ice cubes

Mixing instructions: Pour vodka, sweet and sour mix, blue curaçao, and pineapple juice into a shaker with ice cubes. Shake, pour, and garnish rim of the glass with a pineapple slice.

Pink Passion Martini—drink color: pink

3 oz. gin

1 oz. pink strawberry liqueur (Volare Wild Strawberry Liqueur is a good brand)

1 strawberry

1 lemon twist

Mixing instructions: Pour gin and strawberry liqueur into a shaker over ice cubes. Shake, strain, and pour into a martini glass. Garnish with a strawberry and lemon twist.

Sexy and Single Martini—drink color: bright green

2 oz. green melon liqueur

3 oz. gin

1 cherry for garnish

ice cubes

Mixing instructions: Pour melon liqueur and gin over ice cubes in a shaker. Shake, strain, and pour into a martini glass. Garnish with a cherry.

Peppermint Icicle—drink color: green (winter wonderland theme)
3 oz. vodka
1 oz. crème de menthe
icicle stirrer
ice cubes
Mixing instructions: Mix vodka and crème de menthe over ice cubes in a shaker. Shake and pour. Garnish with an icicle stirrer.

Luck of the Irish—drink color: green (Saint Patrick's Day theme)
1½ oz. green crème de menthe
1½ oz. Baileys Irish cream
ice cubes
Mixing instructions: Pour green crème de menthe and Irish cream over ice cubes in a shaker. Shake, strain, and serve.

Tropical Take Me Home Tonight—drink color: red (tropical or luau theme)
2 oz. dark rum
1 oz. triple sec
1 oz. cherry brandy
1 oz. lemon juice

splash of grenadine

ice cubes

Mixing instructions: Pour dark rum, triple sec, cherry brandy, lemon juice, and grenadine over ice cubes in a shaker. Shake, strain, and serve.

Diamond Princess—drink color: clear

1 oz. light clear rum

3 oz. lemon-lime soda

1 lime slice for garnish

1 cherry for garnish

ice cubes

Mixing instructions: Pour light clear rum and lemon-lime soda over ice and stir. Garnish with a lime and cherry.

Kiss Me, I'm Italian—drink color: red (Italian nationality theme)

2 oz. anisette

splash of grenadine

Italian flag stir stick

ice cubes

Mixing instructions: Mix anisette and grenadine. Pour over ice cubes and stir. Garnish with an Italian flag stir stick.

Kiss Me, I'm Polish—drink color: yellow (Polish nationality theme)

    2 oz. vodka

    2 oz. lemon-lime soda

    3 oz. pineapple juice

    Polish flag stir stick

    ice cubes

    Mixing instructions: Pour vodka, lemon-lime soda, and pineapple juice over ice cubes. Stir and add Polish flag stir stick for garnish.

Kiss Me, I'm Irish—drink color: green (Irish nationality theme)

    2 oz. green melon liqueur

    4 oz. champagne

    Irish flag stir stick

    ice cubes

    Mixing instructions: Pour green melon liqueur and champagne over ice cubes. Stir and add Irish flag stir stick for garnish.

High-Roller Highball—drink color: light brown (Las Vegas or casino theme)

    2 oz. whiskey

    6 oz. ginger ale

    ice cubes

Mixing instructions: Pour whiskey and ginger ale over ice cubes in a shaker. Shake, strain, and pour over ice cubes in glass.

Wedding Potion—drink color: pink

1 oz. vodka

1 oz. peach schnapps

2 oz. cranberry juice

2 oz. tangerine juice

1 tangerine slice

ice cubes

Mixing instructions: Pour vodka, peach schnapps, cranberry juice, and tangerine juice over ice in a shaker. Shake, pour over ice in a glass, and garnish with a tangerine slice.

❖ *Busy Bride* ❖ stop. Steal this fabulous idea. Replace your champagne toast with your signature wedding cocktail so all your guests get a chance to try it. Utilize dry ice and liquid nitrogen as part of your signature wedding cocktail. Take advantage of these ideas and your guests will be talking about your fabulous wedding for years.

After you have chosen a signature wedding cocktail, or created your own and named it, then review your idea with your bar staff or reception site manager. I recommend advertising your cocktail at your wedding with printed signs at the bar or a signature wedding cocktail menu card or both. Both of these items should be located at your bar or guests' seats or both.

Thirty-Four

Ceremony Throw Items

Every couple is unique, so choose something exceptional for your guests to throw as you and your new husband exit your wedding ceremony. Keep in mind that you should incorporate your wedding theme, color palette, budget, and your personal style as a couple into whatever you choose for your guests to throw. Below is a list of ideas from standard to extremely creative that you could have guests throw at your ceremony exit.

Below are the five standard throw items used at most weddings:
- ❖ Rice
- ❖ Birdseed
- ❖ Bubbles
- ❖ Rose petals
- ❖ Confetti

Below are some more creative examples:
- ❖ Sparklers (Fourth of July theme)
- ❖ Popcorn (movie theater theme)
- ❖ Feathers

- ❖ Leaves (autumn theme)
- ❖ Daisy tops (spring theme)
- ❖ Streamers
- ❖ Pennies (Italian theme)
- ❖ Balloons
- ❖ Fake snow (winter wonderland theme)
- ❖ Peanuts (circus theme)
- ❖ Snappers (Fourth of July theme)
- ❖ Casino chips (Las Vegas or casino theme)
- ❖ Leis (tropical or luau theme)
- ❖ Beach balls (pool party theme)
- ❖ Pixy dust (fairy tale theme)
- ❖ Eco-friendly confetti (organic or go green theme)
- ❖ Guests shake beer cans filled with beans (redneck theme)

Thirty-Five

Attendants' Gifts

When purchasing your attendants' gifts think useful, practical, and memorable. Find gifts that your attendants will treasure forever. If you purchase gift certificates as your gifts, you should also include a small engraved keepsake like a monogrammed or engraved key chain. Remember, this gift represents your appreciation for all your attendants' help, time, and money they spent to be a part of your fabulous wedding. Generally, these gifts are given out at the rehearsal dinner. Some couples choose the same gift for all the bridesmaids and a different gift for all the groomsmen. The choice is yours.

❖ *Busy Bride* ❖ below are a few gift ideas for you to use when getting ready to purchase your attendants' gifts.

Bridesmaids' gifts:
- ❖ Engraved jewelry
- ❖ Engraved jewelry box
- ❖ Engraved or monogrammed key chain

- ❖ Massage gift certificate
- ❖ Embroidered makeup bags filled with beauty products
- ❖ Embroidered velour pantsuit
- ❖ Other embroidered clothing items
- ❖ Embroidered tote bag
- ❖ A day at the spa package
- ❖ Embroidered purses
- ❖ Engraved flasks
- ❖ Membership to a beer or wine-of-the-month club

Groomsmen's gifts:

- ❖ Engraved beer mug
- ❖ Engraved shot glass
- ❖ Engraved flask
- ❖ Engraved pen set
- ❖ Engraved cuff links
- ❖ Engraved lighter
- ❖ Engraved jewelry
- ❖ Membership to a beer or wine-of-the-month club
- ❖ Personalized barbecue set
- ❖ Engraved army knife
- ❖ Engraved golf driver
- ❖ Purchase each groomsman's tuxedo

Thirty-Six

Wedding Survival Boxes

B e prepared for any emergency that may arise with a "Busy Bride's Wedding Day Survival Box." Purchase a plain hatbox with a lid, or utilize one you already have. Generally, you can purchase a hatbox, or similar box, at any craft store. Take a moment to decorate your survival box by personalizing it or matching it to your wedding theme.

❖ **Busy Bride** ❖ stop. Your work is done. Below is a list of all the essential items you will need for your "Busy Bride's Wedding Day Survival Box." It's easy. Just buy or find the items at home, and fill the box.

- ❖ Bobby pins
- ❖ Clear elastic bands
- ❖ Tweezers
- ❖ Breath mints
- ❖ Tissues
- ❖ Small sewing kit
- ❖ Mini umbrella
- ❖ Female products—tampons or pads
- ❖ Tylenol

- ❖ Toothbrush and toothpaste
- ❖ Dental floss
- ❖ Hair spray
- ❖ Stain remover
- ❖ Superglue
- ❖ Deodorant
- ❖ Band-Aids
- ❖ Double-sided hem tape
- ❖ Double-sided tape
- ❖ Emery boards
- ❖ Clear nail polish
- ❖ Extra stockings
- ❖ Earring backs
- ❖ Lotion
- ❖ Slippers
- ❖ Flip-flops
- ❖ Perfume
- ❖ Black permanent marker
- ❖ White chalk
- ❖ Dried fruit snacks
- ❖ Hair comb, hairbrush
- ❖ Makeup
- ❖ Cash—no more than twenty dollars
- ❖ Mini bottles of liquor
- ❖ Wedding itinerary
- ❖ Wedding organizer notebook
- ❖ Wedding night hotel information

Busy Bride, help your groom be prepared for any wedding day emergency that may arise with his own wedding day survival box.

❖ *Busy Bride* ❖ stop. Your work is done. Below is a list of all the essential items you will need for your groom's wedding day survival box.

- ❖ Toothbrush and toothpaste
- ❖ Dental floss
- ❖ Mints
- ❖ Shaving cream
- ❖ Razor
- ❖ Facial wet wipes
- ❖ Lint remover
- ❖ Scissors
- ❖ Nail clippers
- ❖ Extra boutonniere pins
- ❖ Black permanent marker
- ❖ Band-Aids
- ❖ Tylenol
- ❖ Extra pair of black socks
- ❖ Tissues
- ❖ Stain remover
- ❖ Static guard
- ❖ Bottle of water
- ❖ Deodorant
- ❖ Cologne
- ❖ Hair gel, hair spray

- ❖ Comb
- ❖ Chap stick
- ❖ Antacid
- ❖ Mini bottles of liquor

Thirty-Seven

Guest Favors

B usy Bride, a guest favor is a small gift given to each guest who attends your wedding. The gifts are given by you and your groom as a token of your appreciation for the guest coming to your special day. Today, there are endless guest favors to choose from. When choosing your guest favor, you need to keep in mind that it must coordinate with your wedding formality, theme, and color palette.

❖ **Busy Bride** ❖ stop. Your work is done. Below is a list of themed and non-themed guest favor ideas for you to consider giving your guests.

Themed Guest Favors

❖ **Busy Bride** ❖ note, when I say personalize, engrave, embroider, or inscription, I mean you should put your name and your groom's name on the favor with maybe the date of your wedding. Don't personalize each item with each guest's name. That would cost too much, and guests would get mad if their names are spelled wrong.

Winter Wonderland Theme

- ❖ Ornament with inscription
- ❖ Bride and groom winter snow globe
- ❖ Snowflake coaster set with inscription
- ❖ Santa, tree, snowflake, or snowman wine bottle stopper
- ❖ Snowflake key chain
- ❖ Personalized ice scraper

Fall or Autumn Theme

- ❖ Leaf cookie cutter
- ❖ Leaf coaster set with inscription
- ❖ Leaf wine bottle stopper
- ❖ Pumpkin with inscription
- ❖ Bottle of maple syrup with a personalized label
- ❖ Pear-shaped salt and pepper shakers

Beach or Tropical Theme

- ❖ Personalized Frisbees
- ❖ Personalized sunscreen bottle
- ❖ Personalized beach towel
- ❖ Starfish wrapped with a personalized ribbon
- ❖ Beach coaster set with inscription
- ❖ Seashell bottle opener
- ❖ Seashell wine bottle stopper
- ❖ Seashell basket with personalized ribbon

Las Vegas or Casino Theme

- ❖ Personalized deck of cards
- ❖ Personalized poker chip
- ❖ Personalized poker chip key chain
- ❖ Mini slot machine gumball dispenser
- ❖ Personalized chocolate coins

Italian Theme

- ❖ Personalized biscotti
- ❖ Steel pizza cutter with inscription
- ❖ Chrome pasta server with inscription
- ❖ Mini oil and vinegar bottles with personalized labels
- ❖ Homemade tomato sauce with personalized label
- ❖ Personalized espresso cup and saucer filled with almond candies

Asian or Japanese Theme

- ❖ Personalized silk fans
- ❖ Engraved wooden chopsticks
- ❖ Bamboo plant with personalized ribbon
- ❖ Personalized spoons
- ❖ Silver fortune cookie with inscription
- ❖ Silver fortune cookie key chain with inscription
- ❖ Personalized white sake cup (for Japanese themed only)
- ❖ Engraved wooden key chain

Country or Wild West Theme
❖ Personalized horseshoe key chain
❖ Cactus with personalized pot
❖ Belt buckle with inscription
❖ Boot-shaped shot glass with inscription
❖ Boot-shaped beer stein with inscription

Pool Party or Boat Theme
❖ Personalized beer koozie
❖ Personalized refillable water bottle
❖ Personalized crystal boat

Masquerade Ball Theme
❖ Personalized masquerade mask

Sports Fan Theme
❖ Personalized stadium seat cushions
❖ Personalized golf umbrella
❖ Personalized reflective armbands
❖ Personalized golf or baseball hat
❖ Personalized visors
❖ Personalized football, golf ball, or baseball

Redneck Theme
❖ Personalized pocket knife
❖ Personalized fly swatter
❖ Personalized packet of chewing tobacco
❖ Two or three cigarettes wrapped in personalized ribbon

Organic or Go Green Theme

❖ Personalized tin filled with seeds to plant
❖ Real mini plants in personalized pots or holders
❖ Personalized box with real flower bulbs inside
❖ Live tree seedling in personalized pot or holder
❖ Personalized reusable shopping bag

Non-Themed Guest Favors

❖ Champagne bottle or mini bottle with personalized label
❖ Martini glass or mini martini glass with inscription
❖ Candy bar or mini candy bar with personalized label
❖ Candle holder or mini candle holder with inscription
❖ Incense gift box with personalized label
❖ Heart-shaped measuring spoons with personalized label
❖ Paperweight with inscription
❖ Cooking timer with inscription
❖ Corkscrew with inscription
❖ Bottle opener with inscription
❖ Champagne flute with inscription
❖ Manicure kit with inscription
❖ Chrome coffee scoop with inscription
❖ Shot glass with inscription
❖ Personalized wedding pen
❖ Cake server with inscription

- ❖ Set of spreader knives with inscription
- ❖ Chrome letter opener with inscription
- ❖ Chrome ice-cream scoop with inscription
- ❖ Personalized ceramic tea bag caddy
- ❖ Stainless steel mini cheese grater with inscription
- ❖ Personalized wine charms
- ❖ Pot of potpourri with personalized label
- ❖ Wild flower seed bag with personalized label
- ❖ Personalized mouse pad
- ❖ Personalized cocktail shaker
- ❖ Personalized porcelain espresso set
- ❖ Personalized barbecue sauce
- ❖ Personalized coffee mug
- ❖ Personalized sun catcher
- ❖ Personalized travel mug
- ❖ Personalized tote bag
- ❖ Personalized umbrella
- ❖ First-aid kit with personalized label
- ❖ Mini screwdriver set with personalized label
- ❖ Personalized jar opener
- ❖ Personalized t-shirt
- ❖ Personalized travel alarm clock

I recommend choosing a guest favor that clearly represents your appreciation for your guests attending your wedding. Make sure it's a memorable favor that your guests will cherish for years as a reminder of your fabulous wedding day.

Thirty-Eight

Marriage License

The process of receiving a marriage license varies from country to country, state to state, and county to county. Generally, you obtain a marriage certificate from the town or county clerk's office, the court, church, state authority, or other area-issuing agency in the location where you plan to marry. The marriage certificate is the license that allows you to get married. Once you're married, it is proof of your marriage.

A marriage license is a legally binding agreement between two people. This license is an important document like your birth certificate or social security card, so keep it in a fire-safe box or another safe place.

If you're getting married in the states, I recommend you start calling to inquire about the marriage application process six months or more before the wedding. Start by calling the county clerk's office in the county where you plan to marry. If they are unable to give you the information, they will most likely be able to direct you to the agency that can give you the correct application information.

The application requirements for a marriage license vary depending on the location where you plan to wed. Below are some of the more common requirements:

Identification is always a requirement. Types include driver's license, social security card, and birth certificate. If either of you are not a citizen of the United States, you may need to bring proof of legal right to be in the United States, like a green card, visa, or passport.

Blood tests are sometimes required to check for diseases, to ensure you're not related, and to check for possible conception problems. At one time, a blood test was required in all states. But today, only twelve states require a blood test be taken.

Marital status is always a requirement. If either of you were married before, you must present a divorce decree or death certificate.

Presence of both parties at the marriage licensing office is almost always required.

Legal age to marry in most states is eighteen, but this also varies by state. I recommend checking the age requirement in the area where you plan to marry if you're under eighteen. Some states will allow younger parties to marry if they have parental permission.

The marriage license fee varies from four dollars to eighty dollars. If a blood test is required, that will be an additional cost.

❖ *Busy Bride* ❖ don't wait till the last minute to get your marriage license. Sometimes there is a waiting period after applying and before you receive your license. And sometimes there is an additional waiting period after you receive your license before you can get married. So don't wait till the last minute. I recommend applying for your license no later than one month before the wedding.

Once you have your marriage license, you can get married. After the ceremony, you, your new husband, and your wedding officiant sign the marriage license. Some states also require a witness to sign. Check for your state requirements. The officiant then returns the marriage license to the area-issuing agency (town or county clerk's office, the court, church, or state authority office) where the marriage license was obtained. It is filed, and your copy is sent to you by mail.

Busy Bride, if you decide to change your name, you will need to indicate on the wedding application that you will be taking your husband's last name. Then on your marriage license you will state your maiden name and married name. After the wedding, you should notify your bank, credit agencies, social security administration, DMV, post office, board of elections, your employer, and other agencies that you changed your name. Your marriage license is proof of your name change.

A marriage abroad will generally be recognized in the Unites States as long as you follow the local laws in the area where you're married. I recommend researching about the marriage license requirements in the country where you plan to marry twelve months or more before the wedding. Make sure you and your fiancé meet all the local law requirements and can legally marry in that area. Then you can start the wedding planning process.

❖ Busy Bride ❖ please note that marriage license requirements often change, so the above information is only a guide. It is very important that you verify all information with the local marriage license issuing agency in the location where you plan to marry.

Thirty-Nine

The Little, But Important, Extras

Sometimes as a busy bride, you get bridal amnesia and forget the little, but important, extras. These little extras really do add a lot of pizzazz to your fabulous wedding day.

After your wedding, some of the items will become your keepsakes that you will remember as joyful memories of your wedding day. For example, your toasting flute glasses can be engraved with your names and your wedding date, so every anniversary you can toast to your fabulous wedding day memories and the many more memories to come.

❖ **Busy Bride** ❖ stop. Your work is done. Below is a list of little extras that sometimes busy brides forget. When purchasing any of these items, you should always keep in mind your wedding theme, formality, and color palette. Because everything must coordinate.

- ❖ Toasting flute glasses
- ❖ Guest book or guest signature item and pen
- ❖ Flower girl's basket
- ❖ Flower girl's petals
- ❖ Ring bearer's pillow
- ❖ Unity candle
- ❖ Candelabra
- ❖ Cake cutting and serving utensils
- ❖ Card box, cage, or keeper
- ❖ Cake topper
- ❖ Aisle runner
- ❖ Money bag
- ❖ Any additional wedding must have items . . .

Forty

Trendy Wedding Extras

*T*rendy wedding extras are just a few of the countless ways you can add pizzazz to your wedding and have your guests talking about your day for years to come. All you have to do is think fun, be a little creative, think "wow," and make it memorable.

❖ **Busy Bride** ❖ stop. Take your wedding from ordinary to extraordinary with these fabulous trendy wedding extras. Busy Bride, always keep in mind your wedding formality, theme, color palette, and budget when adding in extras.

- ❖ Cookie bar
- ❖ Candy bar
- ❖ Photo booth
- ❖ Dessert bar
- ❖ Ice sculpture with signature wedding cocktail flowing through it
- ❖ Cigar bar
- ❖ Caricature station
- ❖ Cupcake decorating station for the children
- ❖ Fireworks display or light show

- ❖ Airbrush tattoo station
- ❖ Characters
- ❖ Clowns or circus performers or jugglers
- ❖ Fortune teller or palm reader or magician
- ❖ Celebrity look-alikes
- ❖ Massage station (like hand massages)
- ❖ Dance performers
- ❖ Interactive dancers
- ❖ Comedian
- ❖ Mimes
- ❖ Celebrity singers
- ❖ Cotton candy machine
- ❖ Casino tables or slot machines
- ❖ Karaoke
- ❖ Carnival rides or carnival booths
- ❖ Popcorn stand
- ❖ Chocolate bar

Forty-One

Ceremony Rehearsal

No wedding should take place without a ceremony rehearsal first. A rehearsal reduces the risk of surprises, helps the wedding party to relax, and gives everyone involved a chance to mingle and feel more comfortable around each other before the big day.

The rehearsal is generally held the night before the wedding at the ceremony site. Everyone listed below should be invited to attend the wedding rehearsal:

* Bride and groom
* Officiant
* All wedding party attendants
* Father and mother of the bride
* Father and mother of the groom
* Scripture readers
* Candle lighters
* Musicians or soloist or both
* Florist
* Photographer
* Videographer

❖ Grandparents of the bride

❖ Grandparents of the groom

❖ Godparents

❖ Out-of-town guests

I recommend sending all these guests a printed invitation to attend the wedding ceremony rehearsal and dinner. These invitations are usually sent after the wedding invitations and closer to the actual wedding day.

During the ceremony rehearsal, the wedding party will practice the processional and recessional. Below is a typical wedding party processional:

1. Ushers or groomsmen seat guests
2. Ushers or groomsmen seat grandparents
3. Officiant walks to the front or altar area with his face down
4. Groom seats his parents and then returns to the entrance area
5. Groom seats mother of the bride and then stays at the front or altar area
6. Groomsmen escort bridesmaids down the aisle
7. Best man escorts maid or matron of honor down the aisle
8. Ushers or groomsmen unroll aisle runner from front or altar area to entrance area

9. Ring bearer walks down the aisle
10. Flower girl walks down the aisle
11. Ring bearer and flower girl sit down
12. Officiant asks the audience to rise and welcome the bride
13. Bride is escorted to the front by her father

After the wedding processional at most rehearsals, the next step is to review the ceremony vows, songs, readings, programs, and decorations. Your wedding officiant will help you, if needed, with any of these elements. Keep in mind that the officiant has most likely married hundreds of couples. So utilize the wedding officiant and his or her experiences to make your fabulous wedding a once in a lifetime event.

❖ 𝕭usy 𝕭ride ❖ stop. Your work is done. Below is a list of all the items you need to bring to the rehearsal wedding ceremony:

1. Wedding programs
2. Practice bouquet
3. Unity candle
4. Marriage license
5. Vendor checks

6.   Aisle runner

7.   Guest book

8.   Maps or written direction sheets

9.   Transportation information for attendants

10.   Toasting goblets for the reception

11.   Cake knife and server for the reception

12.   Seating cards for the reception

13.   Seating chart for the reception

You will need some of these items for the wedding ceremony rehearsal, some for the actual wedding ceremony, and some for the reception. If you bring them all to the rehearsal, then you won't have to worry about forgetting anything on the wedding day.

Toward the end of the ceremony rehearsal, the wedding party will typically practice the recessional. Below is a typical wedding party recessional:

1.   Bride and groom exit

2.   Flower girl exits

3.   Ring bearer exits

4.   Maid or matron of honor and best man exit

5.   Bridesmaids and groomsmen exit

6.   Parents of the bride exit

7.   Parents of the groom exit

8.   Grandparents exit

9.   Guests, starting from the first row, exit

The wedding ceremony rehearsal should be fun with a relaxed atmosphere. So don't sweat the small stuff. Stay cool, calm, and relaxed. Whatever happens, happens. So make the best of the situation at hand.

Below are two examples of a rehearsal wedding ceremony and dinner invitation. Copy these wordings or create your own.

Example One—Informal Affair

Please join Angela and Dougal
For a rehearsal dinner at
7 PM, Thursday, April 29, 2009.
We will dine at the Red Rose Restaurant
325 Bridal Gown Blvd.
Honeymoon, NY 14051
Immediately following the wedding ceremony
rehearsal at
St. Christopher's Church

Example Two—Formal Affair

Mr. and Mrs. Anthony Kearo
(parents of the groom)
Request your presence at the rehearsal dinner in
honor of
Adrianna and Dominic's wedding.
Dinner will be served at 6:30 PM on
Friday, April 30, 2009
At Salvatore's Sicilian Restaurant
25 Princess Bride Blvd.
Bella, NJ
It will immediately follow the wedding ceremony
rehearsal at
St. Angelina's Church
502 Holy Water Blvd.
Bella, NJ

Keep in mind that your rehearsal wedding ceremony and dinner invitations must coordinate with your wedding formality, theme, and color palette. So everything is consistent and creates a balanced presentation.

My last words of wedding wisdom to you, Busy Bride, are three wedding ceremony rehearsal "dos":

- ❖ Do review what height the bride and attendants should carry their bouquets—

high, middle, or low. Decide and make sure everyone looks consistent.

❖ Do practice walking down the aisle. Make sure everyone in the wedding party follows the same pace.

❖ Do let the wedding officiant run the rehearsal. He or she has likely done hundreds of weddings before, so knows the drill.

Follow these tips and you will have a fabulous wedding rehearsal and ceremony.

Forty-Two

Rehearsal Dinner

The rehearsal dinner always immediately follows the ceremony rehearsal. Usually the groom's parents pay for the rehearsal dinner. All the members of the wedding party, their spouses, all parents, all grandparents, all brothers, all sisters, godparents of the groom and bride, scripture readers, candle lighters, musicians, soloist, the officiant, and all out-of-town guests are always invited to the rehearsal dinner. Some rehearsal dinners can include almost seventy-five percent of the guests attending the wedding, and sometimes even more if it's a destination wedding. Traditionally at the rehearsal dinner, the bride and groom give gifts to each wedding party attendant.

Also, the host or groom's parents generally make a toast. This usually happens after the drinks have been served and the guests are waiting for the first course to come. Other guests at the rehearsal dinner may also want to say a toast to the bride and groom. At the end of the dinner, the bride and groom may say a special thanks to the wedding party attendants, family members, and friends who are present.

Forty-Three

Bridal Registry

B usy Bride, I recommend you create a few bridal registries about six months before the wedding. Pick two or more stores that fit your style as a couple. Below is a list of national and regional retailers you might want to register at:

- Macy's
- Belk
- Dillard's
- The Bon-Ton
- Target
- Wal-Mart
- Bed Bath & Beyond
- Pier 1 Imports
- Neiman Marcus
- Bloomingdale's
- Pottery Barn
- Crate & Barrel
- Williams-Sonoma
- Tupperware
- Sears
- JCPenney
- Tiffany and Co.

❖ Gump's
❖ Fortunoff
❖ Barneys New York
❖ Amazon.com
❖ Cuisinart
❖ Kohl's
❖ Waterford

After you have chosen at least two stores, get your groom, this book (for the bridal registry checklist), two cups of coffee, and two Tylenol (for after you're done). At each store, you will most likely receive a scan gun to scan the items you want into your registry. If you register with online sites, just click away.

Below are some "dos" and "don'ts" that I recommend following when creating your bridal registry:

❖ Do bring your groom along when you're creating your bridal registry.
❖ Do create a bridal registry based on the size of your guest list. So if you have a large guest list, create a large gift registry. If you have a small guest list, create a small gift registry.
❖ Do register for gifts with a wide price range to fit everyone's budget.

❖ Do keep in mind your home color scheme when selecting your bridal registry items.
❖ Do check the return and exchange policies of the stores you've chosen to register at before starting your registries.
❖ Don't put items on your gift registry that you don't really want or need.
❖ Don't forget to write thank-you cards to every guest you received a gift from.

❖ **Busy Bride** ❖ stop. Below is a suggested bridal registry checklist. As you scan the items, you can check them off the list.

Kitchen

Glasses and bar:
❖ Ice bucket and tongs
❖ Decanter and glasses
❖ Toasting flutes
❖ Champagne flutes
❖ Wine glasses
❖ Iced beverage glasses
❖ Juice glasses
❖ Tumblers
❖ Old-fashioned glasses
❖ Martini glasses
❖ Margarita glasses

- ❖ Highball glasses
- ❖ Corkscrew
- ❖ Bottle opener
- ❖ Wine rack
- ❖ Bar utensils
- ❖ Cocktail shaker
- ❖ Jiggers
- ❖ Shot glasses
- ❖ Wine cooler
- ❖ Water goblets
- ❖ Beer mugs

Cutlery:

- ❖ Knife block set
- ❖ Cutting board
- ❖ Steak knives
- ❖ Bread knife
- ❖ Chef's knife
- ❖ Paring knife
- ❖ Carving knife
- ❖ Sharpening steel

Cooking equipment (not electric):

- ❖ Covered casserole dishes
- ❖ Roaster pan
- ❖ Stovetop wok and utensils
- ❖ Microwave cookware
- ❖ Teakettle
- ❖ Stockpot

* Sauté pan
* Sauce pan
* Steamer insert
* Lasagna pan
* Cast-iron grill pan
* Grill pan
* Omelet pan
* Fondue set and utensils
* Double boiler
* Eight to ten piece cookware set
* Cast-iron Dutch oven

Bakeware:
* Cookie sheets
* Muffin pan
* Loaf pans
* Bunt pan
* Bakeware set
* Broiler set
* Rectangular cake pan
* Square cake pan
* Cooling rack
* Pie plate
* Pizza pan
* Glass bakeware set
* Quiche pan
* Round cake pans
* Soufflé dish

* Tart pan
* Springform pan
* Yogurt maker

Electrical appliances:

* Can opener
* Coffee maker
* Deep fryer
* Hand mixer
* Microwave
* Popcorn popper
* Stand mixer
* Toaster
* Toaster oven
* Waffle maker
* Bread maker
* Blender
* Electric fry pan
* Electric knife
* Food grinder
* Food processor
* FoodSaver
* Food slicer
* Crock pot
* Pasta maker
* Juicer
* Crepe maker
* Sandwich maker

❖ Juice extractor
❖ Ice-cream maker
❖ Coffee grinder
❖ Coffee urn
❖ French coffee press
❖ Espresso or cappuccino maker

Kitchen linens:
❖ Apron
❖ Pot holders
❖ Oven mitts
❖ Dish towels
❖ Washcloths
❖ Kitchen rug
❖ Chair pads

Serving items:
❖ Cheese board and knife
❖ Salad bowl and utensils
❖ Platters
❖ Trivets
❖ Chafing dish
❖ Coffee butler
❖ Briskets
❖ Party dip trays
❖ Punch bowl and glasses
❖ Cake plate

❖ Coasters
❖ Napkin holder
❖ Salt and pepper set
❖ Tongs

Extra kitchen gadgets:

❖ Utensil sets
❖ Pepper mill
❖ Egg beater
❖ Whisks
❖ Spice rack
❖ Pasta jars
❖ Canister jar
❖ Timer
❖ Sun tea jar
❖ Meat thermometers
❖ Egg separator
❖ Garlic press
❖ Splash screen
❖ Cookbooks or recipes
❖ Mixing bowls
❖ Storage containers
❖ Apple corer
❖ Bag clips
❖ Baking mat
❖ Basting brush
❖ Bottle stoppers
❖ Bread box

- ❖ Cabinet organization
- ❖ Citrus zester
- ❖ Colander
- ❖ Corn holders
- ❖ Dish racks
- ❖ Egg slicer
- ❖ Fat separator
- ❖ Flour sifter
- ❖ Graters
- ❖ Ice-cream scoop
- ❖ Kitchen scissors
- ❖ Sauce ladle
- ❖ Soup ladle
- ❖ Mandolin
- ❖ Pizza wheel
- ❖ Pastry brush
- ❖ Pasta fork
- ❖ Paper towel holder
- ❖ Rolling pin
- ❖ Salad spinner
- ❖ Salad tongs
- ❖ Scale
- ❖ Shelf liner
- ❖ Utensil jar
- ❖ Vegetable peeler
- ❖ Water filtration system
- ❖ Wooden spoons

- Sink brushes
- Slotted spoon
- Soap and sponge tray
- Soap dispenser
- Solid sterling spoon
- Spatulas
- Spoon rest
- Strainers
- Measuring spoons

Dining Room

Formal dinnerware:
- Dinner plates
- Charger plates
- Salad plates
- Dessert plates
- Soup bowls
- Creamer
- Sugar bowl
- Teacups and saucers
- Platter
- Serving bowl
- Covered butter dish
- Candle holders
- Salt and pepper shakers
- Coffee pot

- ❖ Fruit bowls
- ❖ Gravy boat with stand
- ❖ Individual pasta bowls
- ❖ Pasta serving bowl
- ❖ Rim soup bowls
- ❖ Teapot

Formal flatware:

- ❖ Eight-piece place setting flatware (spoons, knives, forks)
- ❖ Hostess set—four pieces (sugar spoon, butter knife, pierced serving spoon, and serving spoon)
- ❖ Serving set—three pieces (serving fork, serving spoon, and ladle)
- ❖ Entertainment set—two pieces (servall and casserole spoons)
- ❖ Cutlery chest

Formal table linens:

- ❖ Tablecloths
- ❖ Napkins and rings
- ❖ Placemats
- ❖ Runners
- ❖ Mantle scarves

Casual dinnerware:

- ❖ Dinner plates
- ❖ Salad plates
- ❖ Cake dome
- ❖ Charger plates
- ❖ Chip and dip platter
- ❖ Sugar and creamer set
- ❖ Soup and cereal bowls
- ❖ Serving platters
- ❖ Serving bowls
- ❖ Sectional relish
- ❖ Salt and pepper shakers
- ❖ Salad bowls
- ❖ Rice bowls
- ❖ Pasta set
- ❖ Gravy boat
- ❖ Dinnerware protector set
- ❖ Coffee mugs
- ❖ Cake plate

Casual flatware:

- ❖ Eight-piece place setting flatware (spoons, knives, forks)
- ❖ Hostess set—four pieces (sugar spoon, butter knife, pierced serving spoon, and serving spoon
- ❖ Serving set—three pieces (serving fork, serving spoon, and ladle)

Casual table linens:
* Tablecloth
* Placemats
* Napkins and rings

Miscellaneous dining room items:
* Vase
* Candle sticks
* Tiered server
* Pitcher
* Divided tray

Living Room
* DVDR—recordable DVDs
* Throw pillows
* Fireplace poker set
* Lamp
* Framed art
* Clock
* Bud vase
* Figurines
* Telephone
* Answering machine
* Video camera
* Camera
* Picture frames
* Photo storage boxes
* Photo albums

- ❖ Television
- ❖ DVD player
- ❖ VCR player
- ❖ Ceiling fan
- ❖ Wicker baskets
- ❖ Folding table
- ❖ Folding chairs
- ❖ Bookcase
- ❖ Chair
- ❖ Loveseat
- ❖ Sofa
- ❖ Ottoman
- ❖ Silk flowers
- ❖ Entertainment center
- ❖ Media storage (DVDs and CDs)
- ❖ Magazine rack
- ❖ Stools
- ❖ Snack tables
- ❖ Stereo
- ❖ CD player
- ❖ Portable stereo
- ❖ CB
- ❖ Computer
- ❖ Scanner
- ❖ Printer
- ❖ Copier
- ❖ Fax machine

Homecare
- ❖ Humidifier
- ❖ Vaporizer
- ❖ Hot water bottle
- ❖ Dehumidifier
- ❖ Space heater
- ❖ Iron
- ❖ Vacuum
- ❖ Fan
- ❖ Carpet extractor cleaner
- ❖ Ironing board
- ❖ Laundry basket
- ❖ Hamper
- ❖ Aroma therapy or sound
- ❖ Broom and dust pan
- ❖ Bucket
- ❖ Garment steamer
- ❖ Mop
- ❖ Step stool
- ❖ Trash can
- ❖ Hangers
- ❖ Storage bins
- ❖ Smoke alarms
- ❖ Fire extinguisher

Luggage
- ❖ Duffel bag
- ❖ Beauty case

- ❖ Carry-on bag
- ❖ Garment bag
- ❖ Luggage cart
- ❖ Pullman bags

Master Bedroom

Linens:

- ❖ Comforter ensemble or quilt
- ❖ Blanket
- ❖ Down comforter
- ❖ Dust ruffle
- ❖ Duvet cover
- ❖ Duvet grips
- ❖ Pillows
- ❖ Pillow shams
- ❖ Decorative pillows
- ❖ Pillow cases
- ❖ Pillow protectors
- ❖ Electric blanket
- ❖ Fitted sheet
- ❖ Flat sheet
- ❖ Mattress pad

Window treatments:

- ❖ Drapery
- ❖ Rods
- ❖ Valances

❖ Blinds or shades
❖ Tie backs

Other:
❖ Bed tray
❖ Alarm clock

Master Bathroom

Linens:
❖ Rug
❖ Shower curtain
❖ Shower liner
❖ Bath mat
❖ Bath towels
❖ Hand towels
❖ Washcloths
❖ Fingertip towels
❖ Body sheet
❖ Toilet lid cover

Other:
❖ Curtain rings
❖ Shower head
❖ Vanity mirror
❖ Wall decorations
❖ Soap dish

❖ Waste basket

❖ Hamper

❖ Waterpik

❖ Thermometer

❖ Potpourri

❖ Tissue holder

❖ Tumbler

❖ Toilet brush holder

❖ Tub mat

❖ Bubble bath

❖ Bath oil and sachets

❖ Soap dispenser

❖ Toothbrush holder

❖ Hair dryer

❖ Slippers

❖ Towel rack

❖ Electric toothbrush

❖ Bathrobes

❖ Shaver

Guest Bedroom

Linens:

❖ Comforter ensemble or quilt

❖ Blanket

❖ Fitted sheet

❖ Flat sheet

- ❖ Pillows
- ❖ Pillow cases
- ❖ Pillow protectors
- ❖ Pillow shams
- ❖ Decorative throw pillows
- ❖ Mattress pad
- ❖ Electric blanket

Window treatments:
- ❖ Drapery
- ❖ Rods
- ❖ Valances
- ❖ Blinds or shades
- ❖ Tie backs

Other:
- ❖ Bed tray
- ❖ Alarm clock

Guest Bathroom

Linens:
- ❖ Rug
- ❖ Shower curtain
- ❖ Shower liner
- ❖ Bath mat
- ❖ Bath towels
- ❖ Hand towels

- ❖ Guest towels
- ❖ Washcloths
- ❖ Fingertip towels
- ❖ Body sheet
- ❖ Toilet lid Cover

Other:

- ❖ Vanity mirror
- ❖ Tub mat
- ❖ Soap dish
- ❖ Shower curtain rings
- ❖ Showerhead
- ❖ Waste basket
- ❖ Towel rack
- ❖ Toothbrush holder
- ❖ Soap dispenser
- ❖ Scale
- ❖ Potpourri
- ❖ Bubble bath
- ❖ Bath oil and sachets
- ❖ Toilet brush and holder
- ❖ Wall decorations
- ❖ Tumbler

Intimate Apparel

For her:
* ❖ Nightgown
* ❖ Camisole
* ❖ Negligees
* ❖ Flannel pajamas

For him:
* ❖ Silk boxers
* ❖ Silk pajama set

Tools and Hardware
* ❖ Chainsaw
* ❖ Power tools
* ❖ Pliers
* ❖ Mailbox
* ❖ Level
* ❖ Ladder
* ❖ Hammer
* ❖ Nails
* ❖ Shears
* ❖ Hand tool set
* ❖ Tape measure
* ❖ Shovel
* ❖ Rack
* ❖ Fire-safe chest
* ❖ Stud finder
* ❖ Screwdriver set

❖ Flashlight with batteries
❖ Extension cord
❖ Air compressor
❖ Generator
❖ Carbon monoxide detector
❖ Toolbox
❖ Work light
❖ Water softener
❖ Wheelbarrow
❖ Power washer

Outdoor—Lawn and Garden

❖ Leaf blower
❖ Hedge trimmer
❖ Grass shears
❖ Air conditioner
❖ Decorative flags
❖ Flag pole
❖ Bird feeder
❖ Electronic bug killer
❖ Lawn spreader
❖ Outdoor lights
❖ Picnic basket
❖ Picnic ware
❖ Cooler
❖ First-aid kit
❖ Compass
❖ Sleeping bags
❖ Tents
❖ Snow blower

❖ Fire pit
❖ Garden cart
❖ Garden hose
❖ Garden sprayer
❖ Grill
❖ Grill cover
❖ Grill utensils
❖ Gazebo
❖ Hammock
❖ Hose reel
❖ Lawn edger
❖ Lawn mower
❖ Canteen
❖ Camping cookware
❖ Garden books
❖ Garden tools
❖ Garden gloves
❖ Patio furniture
❖ Patio umbrella

Sporting Goods

❖ Golf equipment
❖ Fitness equipment
❖ Binoculars
❖ Bikes
❖ Bike helmets

❖ **Busy Bride** ❖ stop. You should start your bridal registry early in the wedding planning process. This is your chance to set up and publish a wish list, something most of your guests will actually review before buying your wedding gifts.

Busy Bride, the last thing you need to do, is to tell your wedding guests where you're registered. If your guests don't know where you're registered, they can't purchase items from your wish list. I recommend inserting your gift registry cards into your bridal shower invitations. Don't insert the cards into your wedding invitations. That's just not proper wedding etiquette.

Forty-Four

Bridal Shower

A bridal shower is a gift-giving party given for you before you are married. Traditionally, the maid or matron of honor hosts the bridal shower. But today, anyone can host the bridal shower, from a close friend to a family member to a co-worker. In many cases, you may have multiple showers with different hosts, such as a co-worker shower, a family member shower, a sexy sleepwear or lingerie shower, or maybe a close-friends shower. The bridal shower is an opportunity for your loved ones to help you stock your new household with all the essentials.

❖ **Busy Bride** ❖ stop. You do nothing here as you already have enough to plan. The hostess does all the work for the bridal shower, theme, guest list, invitations, menu, location, decorations, games, and favors. All you need to do is attend and enjoy. After the shower, make sure you write thank-you cards to the hostess and everyone who gave you a gift.

Forty-Five

Busy Bride's Vow
To Get Buff

For some busy brides, a wedding is the perfect reason to get motivated to achieve the best shape they have ever been in. And the more time devoted to a healthier lifestyle, the better the results. Busy Bride, if you've made a vow to get buff, the ideal time to begin is just after you become engaged, about twelve months or more before the wedding. If you're running behind, don't worry. Just get started as soon as possible.

❖ **Busy Bride** ❖ stop. Below is a list of vows to help you get buff. Of course your first step is to see your doctor before you start any exercise, diet, or fitness program.

Get active. Exercise at least thirty minutes a day. If you skip a day, double the time on the next day so you exercise sixty minutes. Remember to utilize cardiovascular and resistance training to achieve the best results.

Drink, drink, drink. Drink water. I recommend drinking eight to ten glasses of water each day. Proper hydration is one of the key elements to a healthy bride.

Eat healthy meals. Keep in mind that balanced meals equal a balanced bridal body.

Watch the portion sizes. Keep your portion sizes small and eat more often throughout the day. I recommend eating something at least ever two hours. This will increase your metabolism and give you an even amount of energy all day long. All busy brides need energy.

Vitamins. A vital component for overall health and well-being is vitamins. I recommend checking with your doctor for his or her advice on a proper multivitamin for your body.

Busy Bride, stick to these vows and you will look fabulous on your wedding day. Keep in mind that fitness is a way of life. My last words of advice—*life is too short, so don't live to eat, eat to live life.*

Forty-Six

Bachelorette Party

The bachelorette party is the wild night of partying for the bride before her wedding. Generally, the maid or matron of honor, or female sibling of the bride, hosts the party. The bride never pays for anything related to the bachelorette party. The host and bridesmaids typically pay for all the expenses. The bachelorette party generally takes place two to three weeks before the wedding. I recommend never scheduling it for the night before the wedding.

There are two types of bachelorette parties, the conventional type and the naughty-and-wild type. The conventional bachelorette party includes close friends, female family members, the bridal party, and co-workers. Everyone meets at someone's home, a destination location, a few bars and nightclubs, or a restaurant where everyone can enjoy food, drinks, games, and good times.

The naughty-and-wild bachelorette party includes all the mentioned guests above and one, or a few, male strippers. This type of party might take place in a bar, dance club, dance studio, strip club, or in someone's home. Activities might include learning to pole dance, dancing with strange men, receiving erotic novelties (from penis straws to male blow-up dolls), watching men strip and lap dance, and more!

The main objective of both types of bachelorette parties is for the bride and guests to get crazy, let down their hair, and party. The more outrageous and creative the party, the more inspired the bride will be to start a passion-filled marriage.

Busy Bride, the one golden bachelorette party rule for all busy brides is this—never sleep with the stripper, a strange man, or anyone other than your groom. Why risk your relationship with your groom for a stripper or some herpes-carrying stranger.

Forty-Seven

Bachelor Party

The bachelor party, also known as the stag party, stag night, bull's party, or buck's night, is a party held for the groom before his wedding. Generally, the best man, or a sibling of the groom, hosts the bachelor party. The bachelor never pays for anything related to the bachelor party. The best man and groomsmen typically pay for all the expenses.

There are two types of bachelor parties, the R-rated traditional female-body-fetish type and the PG-rated nontraditional group outing type. The R-rated traditional female-body-fetish type of party may include alcohol, gambling, lap dances, strippers, porn, escorts, drinking related games, groom gags, and a vow of silence. At these types of parties, all guests are typically charged a door fee or ticket price to enter the party. The money collected is then given to the groom to put toward the wedding or the money is used to help pay for party expenses or both sometimes.

The second type of bachelor party is the PG-rated nontraditional group outing type. This might include a sports game, fishing, boat party, card games, four-wheeling, paint balling, camping, backpacking, beer tasting, bowling, go-cart riding, or many other group outing activities. These parties don't usually include extremely crazy moments. This type of party's emphasis is on the groom and not so much on getting extremely drunk or female-body-fetishing.

The important part of the bachelor party is that the groom remembers it as a rite of passage from bachelorhood to husband. The number one bachelor party rule is to remind your groom not to get carried too away and thus ruin your relationship and wedding. Don't let him do anything that you both may regret later.

Forty-Eight

Last Words Of Wedding Wisdom

B usy Bride, always get what you want when planning your wedding, not what other people may encourage you to get. Keep in mind when planning your wedding the number one person you're looking out for is you. Watch out for wedding industry scams, don't become a victim. Your wedding day should be a celebration of your love for your groom. Not a show of money. Do not be the bride who is only interested in out-doing all her other girlfriend's who are brides. Never forget the real reason you're uniting in marriage— you love each other.

I wish you and all brides ever-lasting marital love.

Enjoy it, and never take it for granted.

Lightning Source UK Ltd.
Milton Keynes UK

171877UK00001B/137/P